301.18
STE

45170

Steinberg, Rafael
Man and the
organization

DATE DUE			

S0-EPA-220

man and the organization

Other Publications:
THE SEAFARERS
THE ENCYCLOPEDIA OF COLLECTIBLES
WORLD WAR II
THE GREAT CITIES
HOME REPAIR AND IMPROVEMENT
THE WORLD'S WILD PLACES
THE TIME-LIFE LIBRARY OF BOATING
THE ART OF SEWING
THE OLD WEST
THE EMERGENCE OF MAN
THE AMERICAN WILDERNESS
THE TIME-LIFE ENCYCLOPEDIA OF GARDENING
LIFE LIBRARY OF PHOTOGRAPHY
THIS FABULOUS CENTURY
FOODS OF THE WORLD
TIME-LIFE LIBRARY OF AMERICA
TIME-LIFE LIBRARY OF ART
GREAT AGES OF MAN
LIFE SCIENCE LIBRARY
THE LIFE HISTORY OF THE UNITED STATES
TIME READING PROGRAM
LIFE NATURE LIBRARY
LIFE WORLD LIBRARY
FAMILY LIBRARY:
　HOW THINGS WORK IN YOUR HOME
　THE TIME-LIFE BOOK OF THE FAMILY CAR
　THE TIME-LIFE FAMILY LEGAL GUIDE
　THE TIME-LIFE BOOK OF FAMILY FINANCE

HUMAN BEHAVIOR

man and the organization

BY RAFAEL STEINBERG
AND THE EDITORS OF TIME-LIFE BOOKS

TIME-LIFE BOOKS, ALEXANDRIA, VIRGINIA

The Author: Rafael Steinberg is a freelance author and journalist who lived for nine years in Japan, first as a correspondent for TIME and then as chief of *Newsweek*'s Tokyo bureau. He later became managing editor of *Newsweek International*. His other books include *Pacific and Southeast Asian Cooking*, in the TIME-LIFE BOOKS Foods of the World series, and *Postscript from Hiroshima*.

General Consultants for Human Behavior:
Robert M. Krauss is Professor of Psychology at Columbia University. He has taught at Princeton and Harvard and was Chairman of the Psychology Department at Rutgers. He is the co-author of *Theories in Social Psychology*, edits the *Journal of Experimental Social Psychology* and contributes articles to many journals on aspects of human behavior and social interaction.

Peter I. Rose, a specialist on racial and ethnic relations, is Sophia Smith Professor of Sociology and Anthropology at Smith College and is on the graduate faculty of the University of Massachusetts. His books include *The Subject Is Race*, *The Ghetto and Beyond* and *Americans from Africa*. Professor Rose has also taught at Goucher, Wesleyan, Colorado, Clark, Yale, Amherst, the University of Leicester in England, Kyoto University in Japan and Flinders University in Australia.

James W. Fernandez is Chairman of the Anthropology Department at Dartmouth College. His research in culture change has taken him to East, West and South Africa and the Iberian peninsula. Articles on his field studies have been widely published in European and American anthropology journals. He has been president of the Northeastern Anthropological Association and a consultant to the Foreign Service Institute.

© 1975 Time-Life Books Inc. All rights reserved. No part of this book may be reproduced in any form or by any electronic or mechanical means, including information storage and retrieval devices or systems, without prior written permission from the publisher, except that brief passages may be quoted for reviews.
Second printing. Revised 1978.
Published simultaneously in Canada.
Library of Congress catalogue card number 74-23044.

Time-Life Books Inc.
is a wholly owned subsidiary of
TIME INCORPORATED

FOUNDER: Henry R. Luce 1898-1967

Editor-in-Chief: Hedley Donovan
Chairman of the Board: Andrew Heiskell
President: James R. Shepley
Vice Chairman: Roy E. Larsen
Corporate Editors: Ralph Graves,
Henry Anatole Grunwald

TIME-LIFE BOOKS INC.
MANAGING EDITOR: Jerry Korn
Executive Editor: David Maness
Assistant Managing Editors: Dale M. Brown,
Martin Mann, John Paul Porter
Art Director: Tom Suzuki
Chief of Research: David L. Harrison
Director of Photography: Robert G. Mason
Planning Director: Philip W. Payne (acting)
Senior Text Editor: Diana Hirsh
Assistant Art Director: Arnold C. Holeywell
Assistant Chief of Research: Carolyn L. Sackett

CHAIRMAN: Joan D. Manley
President: John D. McSweeney
Executive Vice Presidents: Carl G. Jaeger
(U.S. and Canada), David J. Walsh (International)
Vice President and Secretary: Paul R. Stewart
Treasurer and General Manager:
John Steven Maxwell
Business Manager: Peter G. Barnes
Sales Director: John L. Canova
Public Relations Director: Nicholas Benton
Personnel Director: Beatrice T. Dobie
Production Director: Herbert Sorkin
Consumer Affairs Director: Carol Flaumenhaft

HUMAN BEHAVIOR
Editorial Staff for *Man and the Organization*:
EDITOR: William K. Goolrick
Assistant Editor: Carole Kismaric
Text Editors: Peter Janssen, Gerry Schremp
Designer: John Martinez
Assistant Designer: Marion Flynn
Staff Writers: Jane Edwin, Suzanne Seixas
Chief Researcher: Barbara Ensrud
Researchers: Barbara Fleming, Dunstan Harris,
Doris Kinney, Gail Nussbaum, Fred Ritchin,
Jane Sugden, Lucy T. Voulgaris

EDITORIAL PRODUCTION:
Production Editor: Douglas B. Graham
Operations Manager: Gennaro C. Esposito
Assistant Production Editor: Feliciano Madrid
Quality Control: Robert L. Young (director),
James J. Cox (assistant),
Michael G. Wight (associate)
Art Coordinator: Anne B. Landry
Copy Staff: Susan B. Galloway (chief),
Charles Blackwell, Eleanor Van Bellingham,
Florence Keith, Celia Beattie
Picture Department: Dolores A. Littles,
Martin Baldessari

CORRESPONDENTS: Elisabeth Kraemer (Bonn); Margot Hapgood, Dorothy Bacon (London); Susan Jonas (New York); Maria Vincenza Aloisi, Josephine du Brusle (Paris); Ann Natanson (Rome). Valuable assistance was also provided by: Bing Wong (Hong Kong); James Shepherd (New Delhi); Carolyn T. Chubet, Miriam Hsia (New York); Mary Johnson (Stockholm); S. Chang, Frank Iwama (Tokyo).

Contents

1 | **A Need to Work Together** 7

2 | **A Cog in the Machinery** 35

3 | **The Formal Structure** 65

4 | **Behind the Scenes** 101

5 | **Strain on the Home** 129

6 | **Challenging the System** 149

Bibliography 172

Picture Credits 173

Index 174

A Need to Work Together

Throughout the modern world, at all levels of rank and wealth and in just about every walk of life, there are millions upon millions of men and women who share a common fate. Whether they are factory workers or accountants, bishops or colonels, teachers or nurses or government functionaries, they have committed their lives and part of their identities to one of the vast, powerful, complex and impersonal organizations that produce and distribute goods, that explore the frontiers of science, that inform and educate and govern mankind.

These organizations were created by mankind to serve its needs. Human ingenuity devised them in order to perform tasks that were beyond the capacity of a single person working with his own two hands and individual brain, or of a small group using its own efforts. Only huge business corporations, for example, can manufacture and deliver the multiplicity of creature comforts and cultural amenities that modern man now takes for granted: automobiles and wonder drugs and heated homes and frozen foods and color television sets and newspapers and vacations on other continents.

Complex government administrative structures are necessary to defend boundaries, enforce laws, collect taxes, build highways, deliver mail, educate children and protect the weak from the strong. The giant institutions that guard man's health, extend his knowledge and minister to his religious needs require similarly complex construction. Immense organizations like these are the means by which man achieves many of his most necessary and noble purposes; they are the very bedrock in which modern civilization rests.

All such organizations share distinctive characteristics beyond their common capacity for doing things individuals and small groups cannot do. Size is obvious—but has not so obvious consequences. The members are so numerous that each cannot know every other by name or face, nor can all their labors be supervised directly by one person. This fact requires that important discourse, which can be expressed verbally when only a few people are involved, must be written down.

To avoid anarchic chaos, organized actions must be governed by a set of rules, "the system," which specifies how each operation is to be performed and assigns it to a particular member of the organization, not by individual name but by job category or role. Any one of many qualified individuals can be given the role, for it is the role that matters more than individual human qualities, even at very high levels. The British governmental system, to take one example of a large and durable organization, calls for a monarch; this role can be filled admirably by a man or a woman, as different in personality as Elizabeth I was from George VI. Finally, the interchangeability of people within the large organization endows it with an existence of its own. It becomes a living thing, an organism employing human beings simply as the parts that keep it functioning to serve some large purpose.

Some of the organizations' members join by choice. But many others live the organized life out of necessity, or because entering the corporation or the civil service or the church or the military was the natural, expected thing for them to do. For many of them, organizations provide financial security and social status, and they are happy playing out their assigned roles. Today, however, for an increasing number of organization people at every level in the hierarchy, the material rewards and social comforts of the organized life are not enough.

They talk of the "rat race," complain about being cogs in an impersonal machine and sometimes wear lapel buttons that read, "I am a human being. Do not fold, spindle or mutilate." They seek a measure of personal satisfaction that the organization is unable to provide. And they feel that they have somehow lost their freedom on the organization's treadmill, because the organization commands their work, molds them to its needs, shuffles them around like pawns on a chessboard and attaches to them the labels and values by which—whatever their secret personal feelings—they are known to the world.

Complaints about the organized life have mounted in recent years. The word bureaucrat, which once upon a time merely meant a civil servant with limited, specified authority, has become an epithet to describe employees of almost any large organization. Everyone who has worked for an organization—even the contented members—can relate a favorite tale of bureaucratic inefficiency or organizational oppression. And, at one time or another, most of the social ills of our time, from the decline of the work ethic to the pollution of the atmosphere, have been blamed on the "inhumanity" of organizations.

Large formal organizations are an outgrowth of small informal ones. They trace their origins to the need, as old as man himself, for individuals to band together and coordinate their activities in order to get a job done. The first human societies were organized to the extent that they included leaders and followers—even as in some animal species—and the work was divided among their members: men did the hunting and women, old people and children collected roots, nuts, fruit and berries.

But while the hunters and gatherers were organized in groups, they retained a strong sense of individuality. Moreover, in the hunting bands all the members were known to one another. They not only hunted or gathered roots together, they lived together, shared good times and lean, knew each other's parents, children and siblings. Their relationships were therefore complete; they recognized each other as full human beings, as individuals with personalities, strengths and weaknesses.

Modern organizational society on the other hand slices up the individual into so many unrelated roles that a man has few friends who can appreciate all aspects of his life. His best friends in school may not be seen for years. His employers and subordinates know little of his family and nothing of his neighbors. He may work with someone for half a lifetime and never visit his home. Generally, when he deals with others he relates not to their whole personalities but to one of these slices, and when others insist on judging and valuing him only by his organizational role he tends to feel diminished and alienated.

In a modern civilization the individual is always in danger of dissolving into the function or the status. Man's early hunting forebears faced many dangers, but that was not one of them.

The difference between the rudimentary organization of the hunting groups and the modern corporation or bureaucracy is so great that it is tempting to assume that large and complex organizations, involving many thousands of people, are a relatively recent development. In fact, such organizations have been around since the beginnings of recorded history. These most ancient organizations developed only in certain areas, where fertile river valleys and flood plains favored the development of agriculture on a sizable scale.

About 8000 B.C. some alert food gatherer in the Near East noticed that new plants sprang up where some wild grain had been dropped. Within a few thousand years—a very short time on the scale of human history—other gatherers had planted grain in North China, Mexico and Peru, and people were tilling the soil of every continent except Australia and Antarctica. But they did not go about it the same way everywhere. In Europe, in the Americas and in many parts of Asia individual farming families and villages cultivated small plots of land; their prosperity depended on local rainfall—and on their own efforts rather than on any organization.

But on the flood plains of the Tigris and Euphrates, the Nile, the Indus and the Yellow rivers the water farmers needed came not from the heavens but from the mighty rivers themselves when they overflowed their banks. The annual floods had to be controlled, by dikes to protect the population and by canals and irrigation ditches to channel the water to the fields that needed it. To build these dikes and canals the early river kings mobilized the labor of thousands of people, all working under the direction of a central authority and all fully aware that their prosperity depended on the successful completion of the project—and therefore on their obedience to orders. To function properly these river systems required the absolute control of the entire river, or at least long stretches of it, for it could do no good to open the sluice gates in one place if the

The herd instinct

People think of large organizations as creations of the human intellect, but they are common in the animal kingdom as well. Volvox, a water-dwelling organism too small to be seen without a microscope, is itself a community made up of hundreds of single-celled flagellates that have banded together to avoid being swallowed by other cells.

Self-protection is the purpose behind the group life of other animals. Many find safety in numbers while others divide guard duties and authority among specific individuals. Such specialized role playing is most highly developed among organized insects like the ant.

Each ant performs functions that set its rank in an intricate bureaucracy. At the top the queen ant bears young. Next come the males, and then thousands of soldiers, foragers and nurses. The system has existed for some 40 million years, suggesting that ant organizations are more successful than man's.

Disciplined by bulls serving as guards, a migratory band of some 300,000 wildebeests tramps across the Serengeti Plain in Africa seeking better grazing.

The fusilier fish at right, feeding on plankton in waters off the Pacific's Palau Islands, find safety from attack by swimming in schools that move with precision but are evidently leaderless.

Penguins like these Adélies crowd into colonies not only for safety but for warmth. Individual family units preserve their body heat against the cold of the Antarctic by congregating in a group.

These tree-dwelling Indian langurs live in a troop organized around a strict hierarchy, dominated by the mature males that in turn obey a No. 1 leader.

people upstream had already opened theirs too far and taken all the water for their own use.

Once this system was inaugurated it could only expand, as effective irrigation led to greater wealth and power—and greater authority to organize and command. And what that eventually led to was nothing less than civilization itself. It first appeared some 5,000 years ago in Egypt, the land which has been called "the gift of the Nile." As author Leonard Cottrell has pointed out, however, "it was not 'the gift of the Nile' which made the Egyptians into a civilized community, but the fact that sometimes the gift was withheld."

The hydraulic origin of Egyptian civilization was noted by Herodotus, who wrote: "The priests said that Menes was the first King of Egypt, and that it was he who raised the dike protecting Memphis from the inundations of the Nile." Menes unified Egypt around 3100 B.C., and within a short time, his successors had mobilized all the manpower of the valley to carry out a continuous, coordinated program of building dikes and canals and basins all along the river and to store up the produce of the good years against the shortages of the lean.

Essentially the same kinds of measures were taken in the other great river valleys to the East. The ancient societies of Mesopotamia, Egypt, India and China, writes historian John King Fairbank, were all "organized under centralized monolithic governments in which bureaucracy was dominant in almost all aspects of large-scale activity. . . . The institution of compulsory *corvée* labor by the people at the behest of the government usually became well established. This made possible the construction of enormous public works which still amaze us, like the pyramids of Egypt or the Great Wall of China."

Fairbank goes on to explain a fact of such organizational life: that "once established, a government of this type found itself dependent upon the extension of the same principle of economic control. The building and maintenance of canals for transportation purposes and of highways for transport and communication were paralleled by the growth of the civil service. Scribes and administrators were essential to collect the agricultural surplus and superintend the public works."

These ancient organizations soon developed the features that have proved essential to large-scale operations ever since. Workers were segregated into categories by specialty and rank, loyalty to the group and obedience to its needs were deliberately fostered, schemes for rewarding leaders evolved, recruits were systematically enlisted and trained, and step-by-step promotion was established by seniority or formal examination. Most important of all, perhaps, written records became the controlling force of human effort.

It is no accident that the emergence of the complex organizations of the river societies coincided with the beginnings of history. As everyone who has ever filled out a form or sent or received an office memorandum is aware, organizations cannot function without a means of keeping records. An individual farmer or artisan has a memory. Two traders bartering with each other as individuals can remember their debts and obligations. But an organization has no memory other than written records. The memories of the individuals within it will not suffice, for the organization must be able to function in their absence or after their deaths.

Hence, man's first systems of writing developed in Mesopotamia, Egypt, India and China to record the transactions of the river civilizations. The Chinese written language still carries the watermarks of its origins: the ideographs for "law," "govern" and "decide" all contain an element that stands for "water."

In all these societies the scribes, the few men who had learned to read and write, quickly proved their importance to the organization and became valued and powerful figures. In an Egyptian school for scribes one of the exercises the young men had to copy impressed upon them the prospect of becoming men, whose "names are everlasting even though they themselves are gone," who do not have to perform physical labor, and who wear clean, white linen. Four thousand years later they are still the white-collar class.

The development of writing helped make specialized, exactly defined tasks. Registers and rules dictated how the society would operate. In Egypt, for example, the military chain of command was precisely established and every soldier was trained in a specific skill—as a chariot driver, archer, foot soldier or galley oarsman. The army scribes maintained detailed records of personnel, food sources and weapons stores.

When war broke out between Egypt and its neighbors, conscription agents bearing lists of names ranged the countryside to call up the reserves and enlist new draftees. The Pharaohs levied land taxes according to the degree of flooding each plot received, and a trained bureaucracy fixed the rates on the basis of detailed surveys and censuses. Even the priests held graded ranks and titles, functioning as astrologers, scholars, scribes or singers, and working different shifts at the pyramids so that some were always on duty.

The building of those pyramids demanded an especially complex organization of specialized talent. The permanent force of skilled workers numbered 4,000 at one time, and there were also many thousands of peasant laborers who apparently served only when the Nile flooded their land and they could not till the fields. The experts included masons, quarrymen, artists, toolmakers, surveyors, scribes, priests, overseers, engineers and the men who poured milk under the sledges to lubricate the runners as the huge blocks were hauled up the ramps. They lived in barracks, 10 to a room, earned good wages in bread, beer, onions, meat and salt, and were entitled to the services of cooks and water bearers. As individuals, most could take pride in their craft.

That such well cared for specialists were loyal to the organization, quick to respond to even the most demanding directives, seems understandable.

They appear to have led rewarding and satisfying lives. What inspired lower ranks to obey the organization rule is less easy to comprehend.

For the gangs of conscript peasants whose muscle power hauled the 10-ton blocks of stone into place without wheels or any kind of lifting apparatus, the work was brutal and agonizing. These men could expect no sense of individual achievement. Yet the foreman of one gang, according to a written record, related that they were so happy to serve their King that they "came home in good spirits, sated with bread, drunk with beer, as if it were the beautiful festival of a god." That report may sound suspiciously like the tales of "carefree, singing darkies" in the old South, but some historians think that the peasants believed so strongly in the value of their work and felt that they owed so much to Pharaoh, that they really did labor eagerly on the monuments.

One indication of the workers' high morale might be the unofficial marks painted on many of the pyramid blocks. Some of these graffiti proudly record the names of work gangs: Sceptre Gang, Enduring Gang, Boat Gang. Other markings are intriguing references to the Pharaohs for whom the pyramids were built. "Cheops excites love," says one; "Mycerinus is drunk," says another.

The significance of the graffiti is unknown, but they suggest something

that a bored worker on a modern assembly line would understand: an attempt by men to put some kind of unique personal stamp on their work. It is enticing to imagine that the laborer who noticed Mycerinus' condition and somehow persuaded a scribe to record it walked home that night a happier man, a man who had left his mark.

That, of course, is speculation. But there is no question about the intense and self-sacrificing loyalty that the ancient river monarchs received from their nobles. In the tombs of Mesopotamia there is evidence that court followers ceremoniously accompanied their King to his tomb and there, en masse, took poison, to be buried with him.

As Desmond Stewart, a writer who specializes in Middle Eastern affairs, points out, powerful monarchs able to command such obedience were needed in a society that survived by irrigation. "Egypt discovered a truth particularly applicable to societies that depend on the control of a great river: a central authority able to maintain the canals and to apportion their water is a good, not a bad thing.... The king did not merely symbolize strength, he embodied it as the fount of justice and authority.... It was certainly not the last time that a society willingly surrendered some freedom in return for greatly increased security." Even today, the heirs of the ancient authoritarian civilizations of the East are far more willing to sacrifice their personal desires to the presumed needs of the group and find it more natural to obey bureaucratic orders—are much more amenable to organization life, in other words—than are the descendants of the farms and villages of the West.

Loyalty, of course, was not the sole motive for this obedience then anymore than it is now. To the nobles of these ancient societies, as to corporation executives today, the attainment of rank and wealth was a great goal in life.

Although most posts were inherited, a man of humble origins could rise in the hierarchy—and rate a magnificent tomb—by real attainment or by somehow insinuating himself into the monarch's favor. (When dining with "one greater than thyself," the vizier Ptahhotep advised ambitious young men some 4,000 years ago, "take what he may give, when it is set before thy nose. Gaze at what is before thee. Let thy face be cast down until he addresses thee, and speak only when he addresses thee. Laugh after he laughs, and it will be very pleasing to his heart.")

Egyptian annals tell of one Uni, a warehouse manager of the Old Kingdom who found his opportunity for advancement in the building of a pyramid. So well did he discharge his responsibilities for quarrying and delivering the huge stones that he won rapid promotion and ended up as a royal tutor and companion to the Pharaoh. Then there was the Biblical Joseph, who, though a slave, rose to the rank of superintendent of the royal granaries and was an adviser to the King.

The profession of scribe was the way to advancement for those of common birth, but in Mesopotamia money or influence was needed just to get into a school. One report tells of a well-to-do student who ensured good

The tribal council was one of man's earliest attempts to organize, via group management, for survival. Among the Bakhtiaris, nomads of Iran, such a council still decides major questions. Here the leaders meet during a mountain trek to discuss the theft of a herdsman's donkey. The victim was eventually left behind to search for the culprit by himself. Said the chief, "When you have only a donkey, you don't go to sleep and let it be stolen."

grades—and thereby his future—by bribing his teacher with a feast, a new tunic and some spending money.

Such a stratagem probably would have had less impact in ancient China where a quite different selection process prevailed. More than 2,000 years ago the Chinese initiated an examination system to select on merit not just scribes but also the officials and ministers of the imperial government hierarchy. At its peak of perfection, around 1000 A.D., the examination system was the principal route to power, and the first question usually asked of an apparently educated stranger was how many examinations he had passed.

Tens of thousands of men schooled in literature and the classics—the only formal education that counted—sat for each round of examinations. But appearance, judgment and speaking ability were also evaluated along with literary skills. Only about one in 10 reached the "palace examinations," the final gateway to the bureaucracy, which bestowed on the new mandarin a merit ranking that would largely determine his rate of promotion in the future.

Promotion through the ranks of the bureaucracy was a matter of careful regulation. Advancement could occur only at specified intervals —normally three years. Higher officials were forbidden to recommend a relative for promotion, and no one was supposed to move up more than a half rank at a time.

By the 17th Century the central administrative hierarchy of China consisted of nine full ranks, each containing two half-steps, and every post in the imperial government was assigned to a particular rank. Calligraphers, for instance, held rank 7-A, the Director of the Banqueting Court and the Director of the Court of the Imperial Stud were both 3-B, and the Grand Preceptor of the Emperor of course held rank 1-A. Each promotion brought a larger stipend and distinctive insignia and dress, and also authorized the mandarin to mention and worship a greater number of his ancestors.

Even such a highly organized system as that, however, did not satisfy the Confucian idealists, who felt that it encouraged officials to pay more attention to their own careers than to the service of the Emperor. Sounding a frustrated cry that would be repeated about other civil servants throughout the centuries, the Chinese reformer Fan Chung-yen protested—in a memorandum that scholars have dated as early as 1029—that "in the morning the bureaucrats receive their new appointments; the same evening, they begin to maneuver for their next promotions. Offices are frankly regarded as career stepping stones. Officials, in their mutual self-interest, conceal each other's faults. No wonder the common people suffer so much from maladministration."

With minor modifications the Chinese bureaucracy and examination system survived until modern times, absorbing and taming several waves of barbarian invaders. Faith in the virtues of a literary education, the assumption that the classics encompassed all knowledge necessary for government, remained an integral part of the entire organizational structure—and eventually contributed to its downfall. Absorbed by their bureaucratic way of doing things, the mandarins were unable to understand or cope with the impact of European intrusion in the 19th Century, and they stood by helplessly while the Western nations dismembered their land and humiliated their people.

When the original organizations were formed the kings ruled everything. The Pharaohs, for example, embodied all the civil, military and religious authority. Under them, deputies for justice, religion, public works and the military were considered to be carrying out the Pharaoh's wishes. But within a thousand years or so the Pharaohs had turned over more and more administration to their subordinates. The temples, the courts and the army developed their own organizations and in some cases were able to challenge the Pharaoh—a process not unlike the aggrandizement of modern bureaucracies. The temples, grown fat with tax exemptions and with tribute they received in the name of the gods after every military victory, became powerful enough to send the Pharaoh on new conquests to swell the temple coffers even more.

The proliferation of separate organizations accelerated in Roman times with the appearance of a special, refined one. In the legions of Rome, the world beheld the prototype of the modern army, an organization that remained unmatched for centuries. Earlier Romans, like Egyptian and Greek nobles before them, had furnished their own chariots and arms and had fought as independent warriors with their kings, as the knights of feudal Europe were to do later. But Marius Gaius, who was both a consul and a general, and the Emperor Augustus Caesar did away with that. They opened enlistment to the proletariat, provided weapons, standardized pay and tactics and commands, spelled out the rights and duties of the soldiers through formal regulations, and placed everyone under the discipline of rank. Most important, their system generated an officer corps of experienced, valorous men with proved capacities for leadership—the centurions. This hierarchy of commanders more than anything else enabled the legions to conquer and control an empire that encompassed some two million square miles.

The organization of the Roman legion was marvelously complex. Each of these units, numbering 6,000 men, was led by a *legate*, who was appointed to his post on the basis of experience, which might or might not be strictly military, but every lower command was held by a veteran soldier who had risen through the ranks. Promotion was a complicated process, depending on the ranking of the subdivisions, called cohorts and centuries, within a legion.

Each legion was composed of 10 cohorts—600 men—numerically graded from one to 10, and within each cohort were six centuries of 100 men apiece. The centuries were commanded by officers called centurions, and the senior centurion in each cohort commanded the entire cohort as well as his own century. Moreover, the senior centurion of the No. 1 cohort of

The quintessential symbol of the organization, the written record is as old as civilization—which could hardly exist without it. This fragment of a 133-foot-long document lists employees of Egypt's Pharaoh Ramses III. By his time, about 1150 B.C., records were kept on papyrus, an advance over bulky clay tablets.

Chapter 1

The Chinese civil service was one of the most enduring bureaucracies ever devised—governing the country from the Seventh to the early 20th Century—partly because it recruited talented officials by testing them in written examinations. The examination halls in Peking are represented in floor-plan style in this diagram reproduced from a centuries-old woodprint. The rows of tiny white dots indicate cubicles in which the candidates were locked while taking the tests.

every legion ranked as *primus pilus* (in effect "first spearman," after the pilum, his heavy seven-foot weapon). Not only did the *primus pilus* command his own century and his own cohort, but he also served as a kind of sergeant major to the whole legion and participated in the war councils of the generals.

To reach the exalted rank of *primus pilus* by the customary step-by-step promotion system, the lowest-ranked centurion in the 10th cohort would have to move to the same rank in the ninth cohort, then the eighth and so on. When he made it to the first cohort he would then have to move up one step at a time through the six ranks there. The whole process could take 20 years, but in actual practice outstanding leaders often were promoted rapidly or skipped over some of the steps to join the first cohort and more quickly become *primus pilus*.

The complicated scheme for grading officers is only one example of the way the Roman army organized every detail of military life into a logical

18

system. Little was left to individual discretion or originality. Everything was done by the numbers. Even when setting up a camp the *primus pilus* had to be sure that all the tents and facilities were laid out in a precisely prescribed manner so that, wherever the legion might be, every soldier always found himself in familiar surroundings and could fall in quickly with his unit in the dark.

On the move, the discipline, efficiency and organization of the legions were even more impressive. The Jewish historian Josephus, who fought against the Romans, described how Vespasian, in 67 A.D., marched on Judaea "in the customary Roman order."

"The non-Roman lightly armed troops and archers were sent in advance to scout for ambushes. Next came a contingent of heavy-armed Roman soldiers, infantry and cavalry. They were followed by a detachment composed of ten men from each century, carrying their own equipment and the instruments for marking out the camp; after them came the road makers to straighten the curves on the road, to level the rough places and to cut down obstructing woods, in order to spare the army the fatigue of a toilsome march. Behind these troops, Vespasian posted men with his personal baggage and that of his legates, with a strong escort of cavalry to protect them. He himself rode behind with the pick of the infantry and cavalry and his guard of lancers . . . mules carrying the siege towers and the other machines. Then came the legates, the prefects of the cohorts, and the tribunes with an escort of picked troops. Next the standards surrounding the eagle (which in the Roman army preceded every legion). These sacred emblems were followed by the trumpeters, and behind them came the solid column, marching six abreast. . . . Last of all for security [there came] a rearguard composed of light and heavy infantry and a considerable body of cavalry."

Within a few hundred years of that awe-inspiring march, the Roman Empire had fallen into decline. One of the reasons suggested by some historians was excessive growth of bureaucracies. "The stupendous fabric," Gibbon wrote, "yielded to the pressure of its own weight."

That was not by any means the end of Rome's influence on the evolution of large organizations. The threads of the Empire were salvaged and rewoven into a new, more enduring fabric, the Roman Catholic Church. Adaptable to changing circumstances and differing cultures, embracing scores of orders and ranks and inner structures, wielding tremendous power over the personal lives of both laity and clergy, administering its own sources of wealth and its own educational systems, the Catholic Church is today the world's oldest living complex organization. Furthermore, by establishing a graded hierarchy through which any man could rise to the top and by promulgating impersonal rules that all its members are supposed to live by, the Catholic Church virtually completed the development of modern bureaucracy.

One of the most remarkable examples of early Church organization is the set of rules that St. Benedict issued when he established his monastic order in the Sixth Century. Emphasizing that his monks must repress their self-will in order to serve God and the community, St. Benedict insisted on prompt obedience to the abbot. But, with a touch of bureaucratic understanding, he made it clear that the abbot could expect obedience only to "lawful" orders.

And then St. Benedict proceeded to spell out the laws: manual labor was required for at least five hours a day, certain psalms were to be read at precise hours, specific hours and menus were established for meals, monks had to sleep in their habits so that they could be ready for duty as soon as they arose, kitchen service was performed by all monks in turn, and specified methods were used to select the deans, who supervised 10 monks each. St. Benedict's Rule also established a rising scale of punishments for disobedient monks, starting with private admonition, going on to public reproof and isolation at meals, then to "scourging" and finally expulsion. An expelled monk might reenter the monastery, St. Benedict declared, but only twice: the third expulsion was final.

"Whatever the monk does," Catholic scholar G. Cyprian Alston explained, "he does it not as an independent individual but as part of a larger organization." Seldom in history has any organization attempted to impose such a thoroughgoing control over the lives and activities of voluntary members.

The Benedictine Order is still flourishing, living proof that the human individual can dissolve himself in an organization more readily and willingly than skeptics imagine. And the concepts of systemic operation that the order and other groups in the past evolved have appeared again and again in all the great religious hierarchies, armies, governments and bureaucracies of history.

Through most of recorded history, however, only a small number of men in any society were involved with large organizations; governments like that of China were likewise merely shallow layers of officialdom floating on a sea of unorganized people. Most of the population, in every age and every country, labored on the land and lived in tiny unchanging villages, or toiled in small urban stores or workshops. They knew personally everyone they dealt with from day to day, and they lived from birth to death much as their parents had.

But that society vanished—in the Western world, at least—when the Industrial Revolution began to sweep up masses of men and women into factory organizations as hierarchical and impersonal and large as the armies or the Church. The Industrial Revolution climaxed a train of events. Explorers had found new markets; traders had amassed commercial capital; scientists and inventors had devised new machines and techniques. Entrepreneurs appeared who saw the possibility of tremendous increases in the production—and sale—first of textiles and later of every type of goods. The labor-saving machines were too cumbersome and too expensive to be scattered in the cottages and villages where the spinners and weavers had worked in the past, so factories were built.

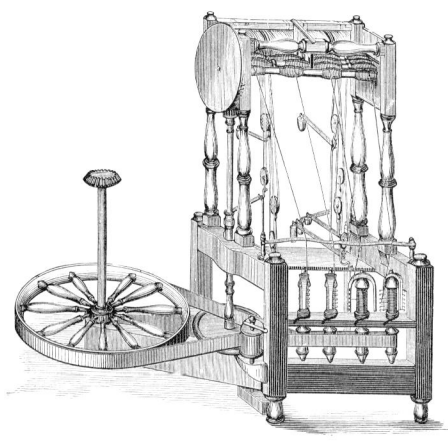

The gigantic organizations of modern industry came into being with the Industrial Revolution, when inventions like this spinner transformed the process of producing cloth in England in the 18th Century. Patented by Richard Arkwright in 1769, it converted spinning from a part-time task to be performed at home into a full-time factory job.

Row behind row of women work at sewing machines in a U.S. garment loft of the early 1920s, an establishment typical of the mass-production factories that evolved out of the Industrial Revolution. Such factories brought management, workers and machines together under one roof, replacing the master-and-apprentice team of the earlier cottage industry with complex organizations of work forces often numbering in the thousands.

By specializing labor and mechanizing most of the steps in manufacturing their wares, the entrepreneurs were able to substitute low-paid unskilled workers for high-paid craftsmen, with profitable results. As Adam Smith reported in *The Wealth of Nations:* "A workman not educated to this business . . . could scarce, perhaps, with utmost industry, make one pin a day, and certainly not make twenty. But in the way in which this business is now carried on, not only the whole work is a peculiar trade, but it is divided into a number of branches, of which the greater part are likewise peculiar trades. One man draws out the wire, another straightens it, a third cuts it, a fourth points it, a fifth grinds it at the top for receiving the head; to make the head requires two or three distinct operations; to put it on is a peculiar business. . . . I have seen a small manufactory of this sort where ten men only were employed and where some of them consequently performed two or three distinct operations. But though they were very poor, and therefore but indifferently accommodated with the necessary machinery, they could, when they exerted themselves, make upwards of forty-eight thousand pins in a day."

During the last decades of the 18th Century and the first half of the

19th Century, men, women and children in England—later in the United States and on the Continent—abandoned the pastoral, individualistic communities of their ancestors and moved to the cities to minister to the insatiable machines.

For a long time these industries were managed by their owners, but as factory ownership spread among many stockholders, and as the operations increased in complexity, a new class of managers arose, as integral to the industry as its machines were. Workers submitted to the discipline of the managerial hierarchy, labored on a predetermined time schedule and performed specialized tasks over and over again. In other words, work itself was carefully organized, just as the army always had been. And as the soldiers of war sacrificed their lives for "glory" or "victory," the new soldiers of the machine were called upon to sacrifice themselves in the name of "efficiency" or "profit."

As late as the 1890s, however, some factory workers in America could still decide for themselves how they were to perform parts of their jobs. Then along came Frederick W. Taylor, an American engineer, who organized this aspect of life with a revolutionary new doctrine of efficiency. In his classic work, *Scientific Management*, published in 1911, Taylor derided the "managers of the old school, who feel . . . it is better to allow each workman to develop his individuality by choosing the particular implements and methods which suit him best."

To Taylor, who regarded most workmen as sluggards with small brains, allowing laborers to make decisions was nothing but folly. He believed that there was an ideal way to perform every factory task and that through time-and-motion studies an expert could determine that ideal method and calculate the time it should take to perform the task. In the interests of efficiency, he insisted, management should make that determination and direct the workers precisely how to do their jobs. Fellow engineer Henry Towne summed up Taylor's philosophy with one sentence: "It is essential to segregate the *planning* of work from its *execution*; to employ for the former trained experts possessing the right mental equipment, and for the latter men having the right physical equipment."

Taylor's so-called scientific theory of management appeared to increase efficiency. But it underrated the human element. A worker purposely prevented from using his "mental equipment" is likely to be inefficient and is almost certain to be bored and resentful. Modern managers recognize this fact, and some are giving employees the opportunity to participate in planning and scheduling the work they do.

Over the past 200 years, as the techniques of the Industrial Revolution advanced, more new jobs and professions appeared, specialization increased, and new kinds of complex organizations were created to deal with the products or the problems of the old. Today government bureaucracies regulate and protect corporations and their customers; schools, universities and scientific establishments produce experts who possess highly developed skills and techniques; specialized corporations market and transport and advertise factory products; huge international banks and investment houses handle profits; unions and professional associations serve multitudes of workers; and many kinds of entertainment organizations compete for their leisure time. In sum, nearly everybody in industrialized nations, regardless of social class, profession or level of education is part of one or more organizations.

All of these organizations, new and old, fit to some degree the classic description of bureaucracy outlined by the German sociologist Max Weber more than 50 years ago. Weber defined bureaucracy as a hierarchical organization of functions in which each office presides over a clearly defined sphere of competence; officials are protected with lifetime tenure as long as they obey the rules; salaries are linked to rank; and recruitment and promotion depend on objective qualifications. Most important, a sharp line is drawn between the office, or job, and the person who fills it; the official cannot appropriate his position for personal gain.

Weber was analyzing government bureaucracies and comparing them to the unreliable and inefficient organizations of an earlier day. He made much of bureaucracy's "technical superiority over any other form of organization." The "special virtue" of bureaucracy, as Weber saw it, is "in eliminating from official business love, hatred, and all purely personal, irrational and emotional elements."

But Weber himself came to realize that all personal and emotional elements cannot be eliminated where people are involved. In a subsequent debate he deplored the "passion for bureaucracy" of some employees, and spoke derisively of "little men clinging to little jobs and striving toward bigger ones." Beyond that, he raised a fundamental question about the quest for technical superiority: "What can we oppose to this machinery in order to keep a portion of mankind free from this parceling-out of the soul, from this supreme mastery of the bureaucratic way of life?"

Much has changed since Weber's day. Organizations have grown larger, and many have become more beneficent and more humane. But the key question remains: How is technical superiority to be achieved without allowing bureaucracy to master the human individual? This is the eternal problem for man and the organization.

Primal cooperation

Public spectacle—as dramatic and theatrical as possible—is a peculiar but essential element of the large organization. From time to time—at an anniversary, a convention or some other special event—many an organization takes a break from day-to-day work and dolls up in its Sunday best.

Just as the Roman legions returned triumphantly from victory, and medieval guilds put on spectacular pageants, major organizations today find opportunities to parade in public with all the splendor they can command. Even generally secretive groups like the Communist government of the Soviet Union allow for this need for occasional public display *(opposite)*.

These exhibits are ostensibly put on to mark a particular occasion, but really serve as a celebration of the organization and what it stands for, a proud affirmation of the entity and the roles of the individuals within it. Though outsiders may be permitted to watch, the principal audience is the participants themselves, for they see their organization brought to life. Its structure, laid out in black and white on the traditional chart, becomes visible in living color, while costume styles, colors and badges place real people in their places in the stratified hierarchy.

On view, each individual can see —and show to others—how his status and identity fit into the whole. If he is at the top of the structure, his outfit and placement signal both his accomplishments and the deference to which he is entitled. A person at a lower level can see the elevations to which he can aspire. And all members of the organization, from top to bottom, can take pride in the strength and purpose demonstrated by their collective display.

In a blaze of red—the symbolic color of the Russian Revolution—thousands of workers parade triumphantly past the tomb of Lenin in Moscow, making an overwhelming demonstration of solidarity nominally staged to celebrate the 47th anniversary of the Soviet state. The marchers bear signs extolling Lenin, the Communist Party and the products of their labor, while their leaders, standing on the tomb façade, acknowledge salutes.

As competition and as spectacle, the International Olympics are the apotheosis of big organization in the world of sport. Here, emphasizing the multinational nature of the quadrennial games, groups of athletes dressed in the costumes of their countries assemble for the opening ceremonies of the 1972 Olympics in Munich. In front of each of the massed ranks of athletes is a long row of girls bearing signs with the names of some 110 participating lands. Circles of dancing children surround the whole assemblage.

In an opulent display of continuity with millennia past, diversely uniformed Iranian soldiers stand at attention during festivities celebrating the 2,500th anniversary of the Persian Empire. From front to rear are troops of the "literacy corps" (men who teach reading and writing in villages), as well as soldiers in 18th Century military dress, army bandsmen and tribesmen of the militia.

A high point of self-congratulation is toasted during a vacuum-cleaner company's 50th anniversary convention in New York City. Each man's status in the organization is as clearly delineated as it is among diplomats at a formal reception. The most honored members of the sales force, each responsible for sales of $100,000 or more a year, wear gold jackets with an "E" for Electrolux and sit with their spouses near the stage. Their less successful colleagues, wearing blue, are assigned seats farther away from the president (left) or in the balconies.

31

Among immense religious organizations the Roman Catholic Church stages ceremonial displays that for pomp and circumstance are unequaled anywhere in the world—even in countries where it is not the dominant faith. Here Pope Paul VI himself (under canopy at right), having made a pilgrimage from his Vatican headquarters in Rome to Bombay, blesses newly ordained, white-robed priests at a great outdoor altar, erected near the university clock tower to honor the Pope's ceremonial visit.

A Cog in the Machinery

A century ago Alfred Krupp, the German munitions maker, spelled out the principle underlying every large organization. He put it quite baldly: "What I shall attempt to bring about is that nothing of importance shall be dependent upon the life or existence of any particular person; that nothing of importance shall happen . . . without the foreknowledge and approval of the management; that the past and the determinable future of the establishment can be learned in the files of the management without asking a question of any mortal."

Such inhuman efficiency can never be achieved—fortunately so, in the view of most people—not even by tyrants as unfeeling and single-minded as Krupp. But his general goal, interpreted more humanely, has been shared by planners before his time and since: to create an organizational structure that would be self-perpetuating, flourishing independently of the human beings who come and go to make it operate. If one man on a Krupp furnace crew quit or was retired or fired, he could be replaced quickly without disrupting work. So, too, could every other laborer, clerk, foreman, engineer and manager—right up to the Krupp family members who, in succession, owned the firm. To accomplish this end, Krupp drew up a *Generalregulativ* that specified the duties and relationships of everyone from managers to office boys. If anyone had complaints he was to go through channels. And there must have been complaints. To arrive late at work by five minutes was punished by the loss of one hour's pay; impudence was punished by immediate dismissal. At one point Krupp even tried to persuade his workmen to wear uniforms—he himself would have been dressed as a field marshal—but he was talked out of it.

Even without uniforms, Krupp established a dynasty that accumulated Europe's largest family fortune and ruled Europe's largest industrial combine until 1967, when the firm became publicly owned. He succeeded because he understood that an organization must be more than a group of human beings; it is a structure of positions that human beings occupy. Even in the simplest organization—a Boy Scout patrol, a sailboat crew —activities have to be coordinated to achieve a common purpose. This coordination requires work to be planned and divided among the members; each must be given a definite position that calls for specific conduct, so that all can predict and respond to the behavior of everybody else. When one man throws a ball, another must be there to catch it; when the boss gives an order, a subordinate must carry it out.

In larger organizations, where co-workers may never meet, the survival of the entire establishment depends on maximum predictability, which only formally structured positions can assure. Each position must be defined and maintained not only in terms of its own functions but also in its relationship to other positions. In such a system individuals—from chairman of the board to night watchman—are replaceable; only the positions are vital and permanent. It is all very much like a play: the characters fill roles, and not in dress, speech nor action are the performers to be confused; the leading lady does not speak the housemaid's lines.

A play must be cast. And the roles in the organization must be filled also —with people. Theoretically, at least, a candidate is selected in terms of how well he will fit the opening, on the basis of what he is rather than who he is. Cleveland Amory underscores in *The Proper Bostonians* the generally impersonal standards involved. He tells of a Chicago firm that wrote to a Boston businessman asking for references for a job applicant. When the reference letter arrived full of praise for the applicant's family tree and fine manners, the Chicagoans answered it with thanks, but noted that the man in question was being considered only for a junior executive position, not for breeding purposes.

Somehow the requirements of the role have to be defined and human beings found who meet the needs, or, in time, can be trained to do so. They have to be identified with their roles in an obvious way—by title, badge, salary or subtler sign of status—so that other people recognize which human has custody of which role; confusion is inevitable if the only indication of power is an imposing bearing and an authoritative voice. Movement from role to role must be allowed for. There has to be a way to find superior individuals so that their talents can be put to use in more demanding roles, just as there must be a way to remove incompetents from roles they cannot handle.

This interaction between individual and role might be simpler than it is if people could be tailored to roles or vice versa, but a precise fit is impossible. The most admirable human qualities often get in the way. What is more, each individual has to fill several roles even on the job, and his personal life involves still others. Conflict is inevitable, and the kinds of conflicts that arise as well as the ways in which they are resolved vary surprisingly, not only from role to role and person to person but also from culture to culture.

Role playing, of course, is not something new in society, nor is it confined to large, complex organizations. A role is simply the behavior that is expected of an individual because of the position he holds in relation to other persons. The word person, in fact, is derived from the Latin for mask, suggesting that even the ancients understood that everyone, everywhere is always playing a role. The necessity of role playing underlies a scene in *Being and Nothingness*, in which Jean-Paul Sartre describes the complicated activities of a waiter in a café: his too-quick step, his solicitous voice, his stiff walk, the reckless, unstable way he carries his tray. "All his behavior seems to us a game," Sartre wrote. "He is playing, he is amusing himself. But what is he playing? . . . He is playing at being a waiter in a café. . . . [He] plays with his condition in order to *realize* it."

Yet complete realization of one role—or one part of a role—may interfere with others. A person's job may demand loyalties to more than one group, as in the case of a factory foreman who is expected to boss his men and yet behave like their buddy. Emotions are not supposed to have a place in organizational life, writes sociologist Wilbert Moore in *Conduct of the Corporation*, because they "interfere with duty, encourage slovenly performance, and provide protection for friendly fools." What the corporation needs instead, he says, is behavior by the book and SOP (Standard Operating Procedure).

There may be conflict between the various roles an individual is called upon to play—the common problem faced by a hard-driving, ambitious executive who does not have enough time or energy left over to be a good father or husband. A diplomat continually finds himself in this kind of dilemma: while abroad, and in public, he must defend the policies of his own country, but in dealing with his home government he must often become an advocate for the country in which he is stationed.

The best role players, paradoxically, face the worst conflicts of all. As a successful individual moves upward to more prestigious positions he may repeatedly have to shed familiar old statuses, along with the friends and social activities they permit. Any change, whether due to a reshuffling of responsibility within the organization or to an individual promotion, requires a certain amount of personal readjustment. But repeated changes upward are harder to cope with because the higher an executive rises in an organization the fewer equals he has, and consequently the fewer are his social opportunities to relax and be himself—to step out of his role.

What can happen to those who do mistakenly abandon role behavior was described by Chester Burger, a New York management consultant. He tells the story of a company vice president, successful and rising fast, who for some reason was anxious about his future. When he ingenuously revealed his worries to a colleague at lunch one day, he instantly destroyed his image of self-confident, invulnerable comer. The other man promptly set out to steal his job—and succeeded. Burger concludes: "If you're not sure whether to say something, don't. Share your anxieties with your wife, or with your personal friends, but never, never to a colleague on the job." A colleague can often be a competitor.

For the individual who can follow the rules and accommodate readily to his role, it provides welcome self-fulfillment and a comfortable life. Even before he joins the organization, the recruit can measure its needs against his. Because organizational positions tend to be permanent, he may be able to plan education to match the qualifications succeeding roles require. Once on the inside, his role can afford safety, security and status. If a person is content with his job, good role playing relieves him of worry about whether he is doing things right and eliminates the need to make difficult judgments. As William H. Whyte Jr. pointed out in *The Organization Man*, "The mere playing of the role of the well-adjusted team player can help quiet the inner worries."

Roles can also insulate an individual from unpleasantness when dealing or working with someone he dislikes, and they can spare him embarrassment when taking orders from those he considers his social or intellectual inferiors. It is not the person he is obeying, but the position that person holds. "You salute the uniform, not the man," is the Army's way of explaining that the military signal of obedience and respect is not subservience. How useful this depersonalization of authority can be was suggested by a 1940s study of restaurant workers. Some male cooks and pantrymen seemed to mix up—almost intentionally—the waitresses' orders. Apparently the men resented being told what to do by a woman. But the trouble disappeared once the waitresses were orderd to stop relaying orders verbally and instead to put written slips on a spike. There was no problem so long as the men could pick up the order, impersonally, from the spike where an impersonal hand had put it. By eliminating direct contact between the men and women, the spike enabled them to take refuge in their roles and to deal with one another in a way they would not have tolerated as individuals.

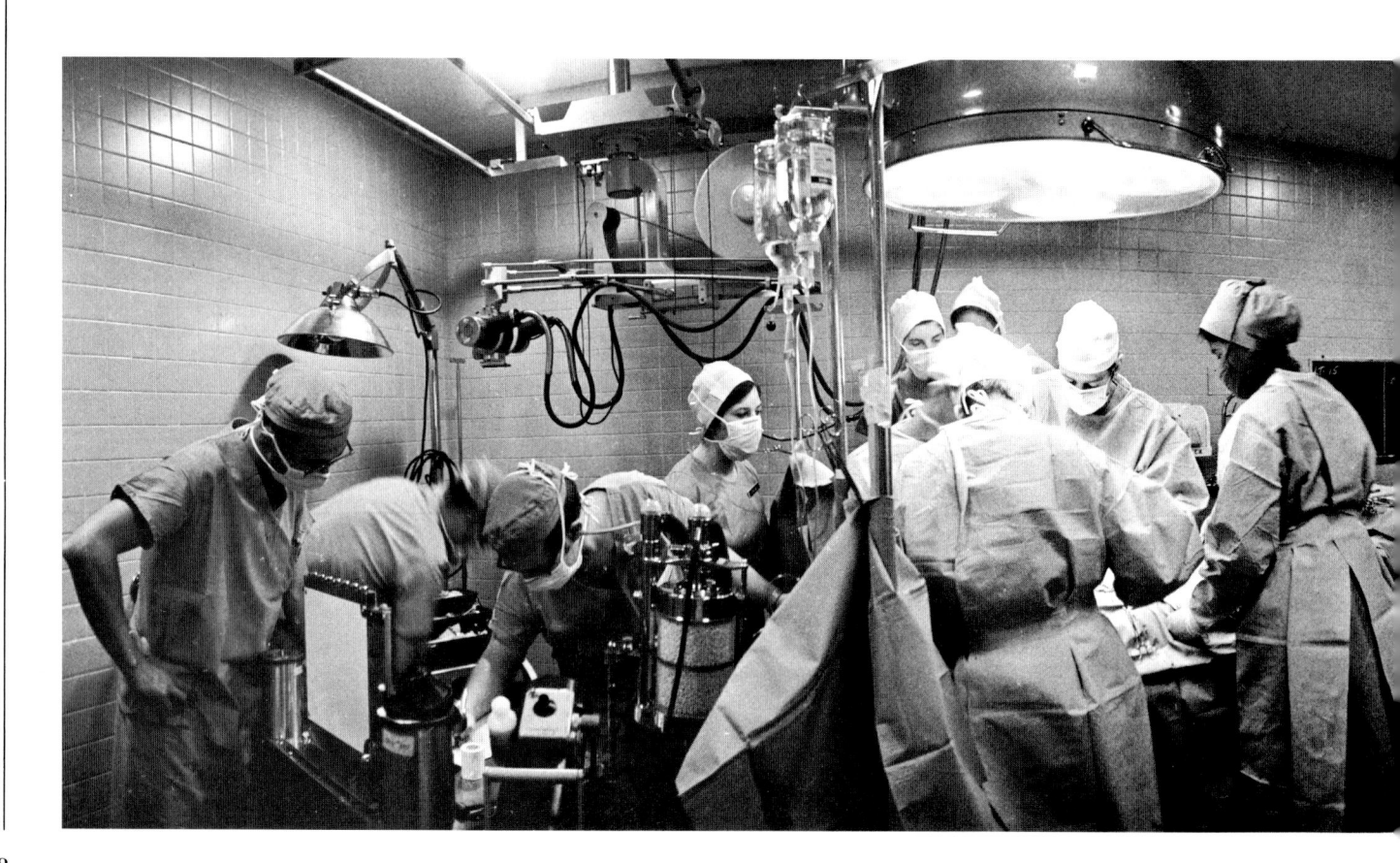

Such tricks for depersonalizing authority are seldom necessary because the role itself usually serves this function. Position in a chain of command comes with the role, determining who its bearer takes orders from and who takes orders from him. This specification of rank is, of course, essential to the smooth operation of the organization, since it enables decisions to be made and carried out with a minimum of confusion. But rank is also one of the chief benefits (or drawbacks, depending on the position and point of view) that a role brings to an individual. It establishes his status in society—explicitly within the organization and very often implicitly outside it.

Although the concept of rank is fundamental to organized life, its application varies widely. Rank may be obvious—in the military services or the Roman Catholic Church—or so concealed that it can be perceived only by a few insiders, as it is among behind-the-scenes power brokers who influence governmental actions. In Western societies—particularly in the United States—its signs may be subtle and its use flexible. In Japan, on the other hand, public and private business is rigidly regulated by protocol based on rank.

In a Japanese corporation or government bureau everyone addresses his superior by title or rank, Honorable Section Chief, Honorable Managing Director. Names are used only when talking to subordinates or equals, and equals rate more polite verbs and pronouns than subordinates do. Every Japanese corporate employee, down to the level of factory foreman, carries name cards bearing his company name and address and, most important, his rank. The cards serve a vital purpose: Japanese cannot talk properly or politely to one another unless everyone involved knows his relative rank and status.

Watch two Japanese businessmen meeting as strangers in circumstances where neither knows which of them takes precedence—at a corporation reception, for instance. If no one introduces them, they will try to avoid conversation. If forced to converse, they will immediately whip out their name cards for exchange, murmuring their company names and their own names, and bowing slightly. Within a second or two each will have read the other's card, noted the rank and calculated the value of the rank in terms of the size and importance of the company. Then, unless they judge their status to be approximately equal, the tableau will swiftly change. One of them will bow again, more deeply; his voice will soften and he will shift to a politer syntax. If both are waiting for something, to get to the bar, for instance, and if the junior is profoundly outranked, he may insist the other man go first. Meanwhile, the superior will have acknowledged the deep bow with a shallow one, or perhaps just a nod; his voice and phrasing will shift too, to a harder, more direct manner and his sentences will get shorter. He accepts the deference, for it is his due.

For a Westerner, there are two fascinating aspects to this performance. First of all, there never seems to be any doubt, once the cards are exchanged, about who outranks whom, and by how deep and how long a

A microcosm of the smoothly functioning organization, a medical team performs a major operation at the Hospital of the University of Pennsylvania. From head surgeon and anesthetist to nurses, each of the 10 persons has a crucial, explicitly defined role, and must carry it out with perfect timing and harmony.

Chapter 2

In an environment almost Kafkaesque in its impersonality, scores of men and women punch out statistics at the United States Social Security headquarters in Baltimore. Such large groups performing similar tasks are vital to the smooth operation of government and other highly structured, complex organizations; but it is the tasks, not the individuals assigned to work at them, that are irreplaceable.

bow. Second, the recognition of their differing statuses, far from inhibiting discourse, actually encourages it. Only when a relationship is clear, with uncertainty and the possibility of a social gaffe removed, can significant conversation take place. The two unequals will never become buddies, but as long as the forms are observed, as long as both play their roles properly, they can conduct business or pass the time of day or even share a ride home in a taxicab.

The egalitarian tradition of the United States protects Americans from such naked flaunting of rank and status, but it gets them into other kinds of trouble. Because Americans feel that they are just as good as those set above them, they connive and angle for prestige in a way that would not only be considered bad form but would be futile in Japan, where status is clearly established. An American often suspects that his subordinates feel equal to him—and fears that they may be right. Thus he sometimes guards his status and privileges so jealously that he may fail to perform his duties rationally and effectively. Paradoxically, the egalitarian society's half-suppressed concern with rank undermines bureaucratic efficiency in a way early writers failed to foresee.

The United States represents the extreme opposite of the Japanese practice. But in many countries there is an ambivalence toward rank, most apparent in the way status is publicly identified. In military, church and academic organizations, titles are routine forms of address, and badges signifying rank may be worn on clothing. The Pope's red velvet and ermine cape, the cardinal's red hat, the bishop's purple cassock, jeweled ring and silver crosier are accepted and familiar insignia of the Catholic hierarchy. Like an admiral's gold braid, they proclaim status and authority in a way no member of the organization can miss.

With this open acknowledgment of rank goes a willingness to accept appropriate perquisites. Particularly in the military establishment—where discipline requires that everyone be able to tell at a glance whom to obey, and be prepared to obey automatically—exaggerated trappings and panoply are taken for granted. The private aircraft and honor guards for generals; the British Army general-officers' house staff; the separate clubs for officers, noncoms and enlisted men; the deference the wives of officers expect from the wives of lower-ranking servicemen—all are part of normal routine and long-standing tradition.

The Western organizations that encourage the display of status are mainly ancient ones, following traditional customs. More generally the flaunting of rank is discouraged in the West. Business cards may be exchanged, but as a convenient notation of name and address rather than to establish title. A bank clerk's clothes look exactly like the managing director's, from a distance, differing only in the quality of material and tailoring. Titles are used in formal address on the Continent, particularly in Germany—where an important man may be referred to as *Herr Verwaltungsgerichtoberinspektor* (senior court inspector)—but less often in England and still less in the United States. Many American executives insist on being called by their first names and take pride in working in shirt sleeves. Yet such modesty is to a great extent a screen. In every organization in every culture, badges of rank exist, proudly displayed and even fought over, as clear a sign of prestige and authority as the stripes on a Naval officer's sleeve—to those who know where to look.

Whether insignia are officially ordained—as, for example, the fresh flowers in the president's office—or emerge unofficially as do the differences in hair styling among different ranks of workers, these status symbols reinforce the prestige of the organization role both within the group and outside. Like the military and the Church, other organizations distribute such symbols most generously to the top echelons.

"A Title on the Door Rates a Bigelow on the Floor," an American carpet company advertised some years ago; by now so many offices have carpets that the color and thickness of the rug are the key to status. For many years the carpeting in the office of the U.S. Secretary of State was blue. One floor below, the assistant secretaries had green carpets and a floor below that, the office directors worked in offices with gray rugs. In every gray-rug office hung a black-and-white photograph of the President, but the pictures in the offices of the Secretary of State and assistant secretaries were in color.

Every executive's office at the New York headquarters of the Chase Manhattan Bank displays a fine original oil painting provided by the bank but selected by the occupant to reflect his personal taste. The value of the painting, however, is precisely determined according to the executive's rank. The practice has been that when he gets a promotion, he is taken to the bank's private collection and allowed to choose a work from the appropriate price range. If he already has one painting, he does not have to give it up for a new and costlier one, but he cannot add a second—unless his new role and rank allow for the value of both.

A more common symbol of rank is the desk, which gets bigger and fancier as its occupant goes up the line, changing from utilitarian steel to walnut and chrome, to mahogany, to Chippendale—until at the highest levels are the executives for whom no desk is big enough and who therefore use no desk at all. They let their secretaries and executive assistants take care of the documents and the paper clips, and they seem to be saying, "This whole establishment is my desk."

Rank can also be ascertained by the presence or absence of a secretary, by whether the secretary shares the boss's office or sits outside it in her own work-space, by how elegantly the secretary dresses or speaks. In New York City, some years back, a secretary with a cultured English accent was almost a requirement in the executive suite—while at the same time one-up Japanese executives were insisting on being chauffeured around Tokyo by female drivers.

The place an employee parks his car, whether he washes his hands in the common lavatory or in the executive washroom or in a private bathroom attached to his own office, whether his visitors sit on an upholstered

continued on page 47

Beginning basic training, a panting Marine recruit jogs around boot-camp grounds with a 77-pound loaded sea bag. He is flanked by drill instructors who continually pepper him with insults.

The marines: total commitment

From the moment a youth enters "boot camp" at Parris Island, South Carolina, he undergoes 11 weeks of indoctrination to mold him into the elite military organization he has joined—The United States Marine Corps. During this time he is regimented and even bullied for a purpose: to submerge his individuality in group discipline and team spirit. The Corps dresses him and makes him act exactly like his fellows. He must learn to play, dependably and loyally, his role in a Marine fighting unit.

The men responsible for his transformation are the "DIs," Marine drill instructors, three of whom are assigned to each platoon of 75 recruits. One is at the recruit's side during virtually every waking hour, prodding him to obedience with a stream of gruff epithets. In every activity, from calisthenics to rifle practice, platoon members who fail to "shape up" are singled out for criticism. Those who try to think or act for themselves are told off in front of their comrades and often put through one-day "motivation" courses—excruciating forced marches. After hours of wading in mud and crawling under barbed wire, few men fail to get the idea —the unit, not the individual, counts.

In the last week of boot camp, restrictions are eased. By then, if the DI has done his job, each man believes, heart and soul, that "what's good for the platoon is good for me." Another group of leathernecks has been made fit for the Marine Corps.

After being relieved of all personal belongings—the only exceptions are his wallet and wedding band—a young Marine recruit undergoes his first physical reformation, the shaving of his head.

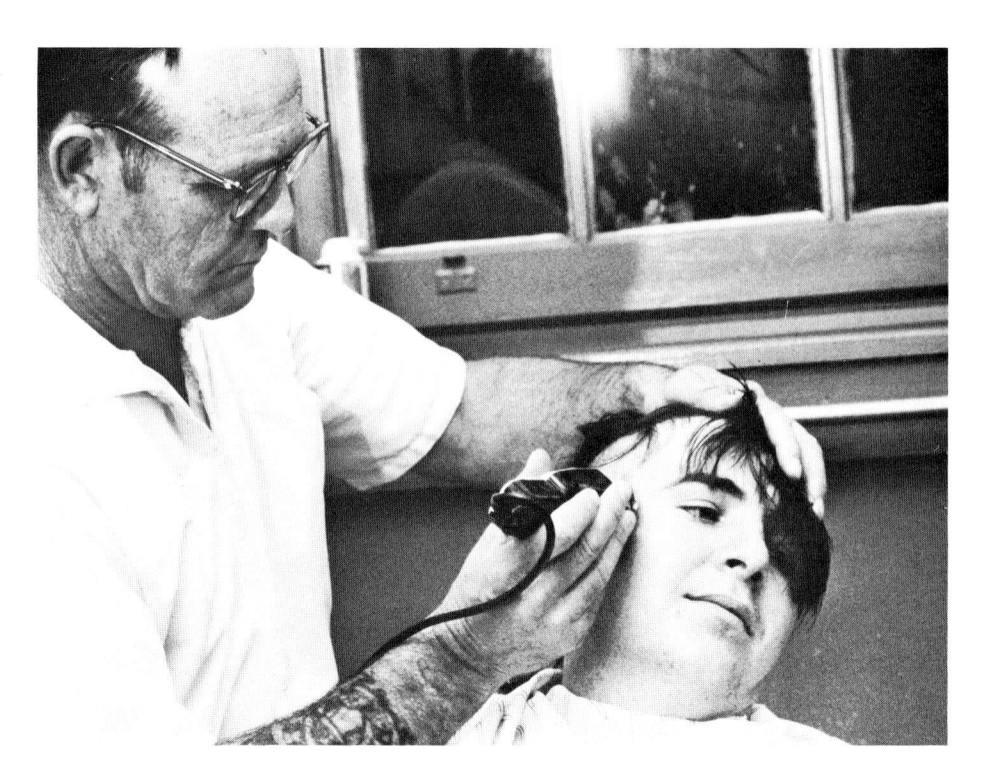

Even their postures uniform, recruits stand in file, silent and naked, after receiving X-rays, blood tests and immunization shots.

Recruits practice aggressive and self-protective skills needed for hand-to-hand combat watched by two drill instructors. The contestants, protected by helmets and pads, are jolted but do not get hurt.

Taken over by his role, the Marine becomes a number in Corps records—one fighting man of known loyalty, bravery and skill.

couch or hard chairs, the number of telephone extensions assigned to him, and how far down the table from the top man he sits during staff meetings —all of these announce rank. If the official organization tries to eliminate such symbols, its members may invent unofficial ones. When a Boston publishing house put all its employees in one big room, the size of each desk, and the spaces between desks were meticulously graded by the staff itself. After someone was transferred or promoted, the desks would be quietly shifted a few inches in one direction or another in order to reflect the revised pecking order.

Like Army insignia, these informal badges must be jealously guarded by their owners. In sociologist Robert Merton's words, an official's "emotional dependence upon bureaucratic symbols and status" leads him to defend those symbols as if they possessed moral value. One reason is that they are subject to depreciation as the corporation spawns new divisions and dispenses titles and other symbols more widely. (At one time Firestone Tire and Rubber had 72 presidents, IBM had seven, and Borg-Warner had 40 presidents or chairmen.) When that kind of proliferation occurs, new and more luxurious badges have to be invented. And of course such badge currency can be devalued as well as inflated. After one promoted executive declined to exchange his low-rank company Buick for a high-rank company Cadillac, the firm's entire system of automotive promotion slipped down one notch; no one under him in the hierarchy could expect a promotion to bring a larger car either.

The most important badge of rank, however, would seem to be the paycheck—at least in a system of free competition for jobs. Presumably an individual's salary ought to reflect his importance to the organization and thus his status within it. Yet this simple relationship does not always exist. People doing the same work and filling identical roles may get different pay, and many a supervisor earns less than some of his subordinates. There are a number of reasons for salary disparities. One of them is secrecy.

Why corporate white-collar salaries are generally discussed behind closed doors is a fascinating question. In government bureaucracies and in the military, pay generally coincides with grade and is a matter of public record. The hourly wage rate of millions of factory workers is determined by union negotiations and reported in the newspapers. But within management ranks, and in fact for nearly everyone who works in an office, salary is discussed only among the employee, his supervisor and the personnel department. Few people will volunteer their salaries, and it is considered impolite to ask.

Wilbert Moore takes a cynical view of this secrecy. He believes it is "designed to obscure an inequitable system of rewards and to protect those who determine salaries from the crude force of competition among subordinates. The man who is given a salary raise or bonus that is not given to his peers is commonly sworn to secrecy or at least told that 'this is confidential.' There is no reason at all for this if the difference in rewards reflects differences in merit by commonly accepted criteria. It is the uncertainty of the criteria of merit or the patent unfairness of income differences that prompts deliberate concealment or obfuscation. . . ."

But among executives, and indeed among many lesser white-collar workers, no "commonly accepted criteria" will apply with justice to all cases except where job proficiency can be measured in numbers, as is the case with a salesman or an investment analyst. There are too many unmeasurable factors involved, ranging from the diligence of a lowly telephone operator in tracking down a traveling executive to the ability of that executive—by a web of subtle gestures and phrases and minor decisions—to inspire the best work from his staff. Two people doing the same job, apparently playing the same sort of role, may earn different salaries because management has decided that one of them is abler or of greater potential value to the company. New recruits from outside the organization or from other divisions within it often may be attracted with higher salaries than those of the old hands alongside whom they will work. And an employee who is promoted rapidly through several ranks may have to wait a while before his salary catches up with his title. The secret salary therefore, although it undoubtedly redounds to the benefit of the organization, also seems to be a clear sign that individuals still count for something at certain levels of the corporate structure.

Seen in that light, the visible badges of role take on a new meaning. They are bestowed not only to broadcast an employee's worth but, when given instead of raises, may conceal the fact that an employee is not worth all that much. British sociologist David Lockwood points out that elegant-sounding titles are recognized by those expert in human relations as an inexpensive way to keep a staff content; who would not prefer to be called a secretary rather than a shorthand-typist, an analyst rather than a clerk? The individual who knows he is well paid can be confident that the whole world sees how good he is; and the fellow who feels underpaid can at least take comfort from the fact that the new paintings hanging in his office seem to impress his visitors and his staff.

Status symbols, even raises, may represent no more than the icing on the cake to many organizational role players. For them the most important incentive is the power that a role bestows on its incumbent, and they struggle for promotion to ever more exalted status, not to enjoy its richer trappings but to exercise its greater power. This drive for advancement serves the organization's purpose, too, for its survival depends on the talent at the top, and the highest positions are the most difficult to fill. Relatively simple tests of skill and evaluations of personality may serve to select good production workers and clerks, and an occasional misfit is easily removed. But deciding who should get an opportunity to manage a factory or direct a governmental department involves fine judgment, grave risks and considerable planning.

In recent years a number of forward-looking organizations have developed ingenious methods of deciding who will get high executive roles.

Instead of using psychological tests to find supposedly suitable personality types, as was the vogue after World War II, the new techniques set up situations simulating the real-life operations of an organization and test would-be executives for their ability to make the right decisions. In one of these "games," a group of five or six candidates is told to manage a fictitious toy company and increase its profits. Facts on the company and its market are presented to the group, but no one is put in charge and no procedural rules are laid down. Every few minutes the testers raise the pressure by announcing a change in costs or in competitors' prices. The assessors observe who takes charge of the group, who cooperates, who panics or gets confused as time runs out, and who operates coolly and flexibly under pressure.

In an even more grueling assessment game, an individual plays at filling in for a supervisor in an emergency. He is handed an in-basket full of memos and letters and given a fixed time to answer them all. The testers look for the candidate who sets priorities, spots connections between related items, seeks expert advice when necessary and delegates lesser matters to his staff. Sometimes, buried near the bottom of the pile, lies a note from the supervisor's secretary reminding him she has left on vacation; the candidate, who may already have delegated certain matters to her, must then decide whether to spoil her vacation and call her back, thus testing still another facet of his judgment.

Such testing games can be used either to select employees to be hired from outside the organization or to be promoted from within. When a role is to be filled only by promotion, simulation is not necessary. The test can be real. Sometimes the competition between those striving for advancement has nothing to do with the real aims of the company, and this approach may be dangerous. Cornered, fighting for survival, the individual may not compete merely by doing the best job he knows how; he may use every trick he can think of, including deceit and sabotage, to defeat his rival —and that might harm the organization. As Moore has noted, "The large corporation is spending some portion of its man-hour resources in internal war and its containment rather than in furthering its various stated objectives." Moreover, Chester Burger, the management consultant, views such power displays as potentially destructive. He believes that intense internal rivalry almost always begins at the top. The boss encourages competition in the belief that he will get the best work out of his employees by forcing them to struggle against one another.

Burger cites the example of a fierce and counterproductive rivalry between a production manager and a plant manager at a New England shoe factory. The senior man, Thea, had little to do besides supervising his very competent junior, Weiner. Thea, anxious to hold on to his job until he reached retirement age, made it his business to find fault with Weiner, and he tried to convince corporate headquarters that the younger man needed his expert help. Since Weiner was actually doing a good job, Thea invented problems, compounded minor ones and constantly criticized his

Chapter 2

Hands folded strategically in his lap, self-confidence on his face, President Habib Bourguiba of Tunisia sits in a conference room on a state visit to West Germany, the epitome of authority and power. Surrounding him, members of his staff play their subordinate roles, standing attentively with hands behind backs, acknowledging Bourguiba's higher rank.

subordinate, who of course had to counterattack. When the chief executive, in another city, was asked why he permitted such a clash to continue, he laughed. He admitted he had planned it that way. "We don't need two men there anyway," he told Burger. "Thea's got two years to go until retirement and I don't want to fire him now without a good reason. Weiner is a good man, but I decided it wouldn't hurt if I threw him into the pit with Thea and let the two of them fight it out. If Weiner isn't tough enough to handle himself, he doesn't deserve the top job. Either way, the company will come out ahead. I'll have a good excuse to force out Thea two years early and get rid of dead wood. Or I'll discover that Weiner is too weak to head up the plant, and I'd rather discover that *before* I give him the job instead of afterwards."

The competition that results from situations like this, according to corporate ideology, "divides the men from the boys." It also produces some other divisions. At one extreme are what Wilbert Moore calls the strainers, the ambitious young organization men "who keep alert, look smart, avoid missteps, and attempt to show up well on assignments or in group policy discussion. They have ideas if requested and otherwise find cogent reasons for supporting the wisdom of the boss's ideas. They learn golf, join the right clubs, think the right thoughts. Their wives are attractive but not brazen, entertain the right people, and suggest that John is brilliant as well as hard-working, a dedicated corporate servant but also a wonderful husband and father."

If the strainers are climbing a ladder, others whom Moore calls secure mobiles are on an escalator. They may not reach the heights that some strainers attain, but with considerably less struggle and fewer tensions they rise fairly high in their organizations, "not by doing nothing but also not by doing anything exceptional." Usually they can be found among the ranks of the professionals within management. "They may be ambitious," Moore relates, "but generally not for the power. . . . They do not spurn money, but [accept it] as payment for doing what they are doing and not for something else."

One problem for the escalator rider, or for anyone who enters an organization vowing just to do a good job and not get involved in the rat race, is that industrialized society brands anyone who doesn't aim for the top as a quitter. He is likely to be passed over repeatedly. And when bright young people press from below for promotion, his superiors may decide he is not the best person for his role. Then he is simply removed. There are now as many ways of getting the wrong people out of roles as there are of trying to get the right ones in.

No matter how it is accomplished, the experience of losing a job is traumatic. To relieve the pain some organizations have developed firing techniques to devious art. Chester Burger counsels managers never to use the word fired, suggesting "relieved of duty" or "terminated" as better terms. With similar tact, an American civil servant is not discharged but is "selected out." Most corporate executive firings are presented publicly as resignations or early retirements to save face for all. The victim may be permitted to keep a desk and secretary and to receive calls at the office for many weeks so that he can preserve the façade of employment while he seeks another job. Some managers find it so difficult to fire a subordinate that they hire consultants to wield the ax for them. One company president who could not face up to the task of firing a vice president directly sent him a memo instead. The vice president simply ignored the memo and his boss was too embarrassed to bring up the ugly matter again; the vice president remained in his job.

Undoubtedly the most uncivilized firing technique was dreamed up by a firm that announced it was moving corporate headquarters from New York to Texas. The notice declared that everyone would be informed on the following Monday whether he was being invited to move or would be left behind to wind up affairs at the old headquarters. It also stated, almost as an afterthought, that executives wanting to know which group they were in could call a special telephone number on Saturday. Naturally everyone phoned, and the unlucky ones got the final word from an impersonal answering-service operator, who reported that not only were they not going to Texas but read a message saying, "The personnel department will be in touch with you by mail; you won't have to go into your office on Monday. They'll make arrangements to deliver all your personal effects. I'm sorry. Thank you for calling. Goodbye."

The opposite extreme, however, can be nearly as dehumanizing for the individual who feels trapped in an organizational role. In corporations where incompetent executives are not fired but kicked upstairs, where goodwill and camaraderie are the order of the day, the individuals can become, in the words of writer Alan Harrington, "trapped in a labyrinth of benevolence." Eloquently describing his short career in one such establishment, which he calls The Crystal Palace, Harrington writes:

"A mighty fortress is our Palace; I will not want for anything. I may live my days without humiliation. I will not be fired. It nourishes my self-respect. I am led along the paths of righteousness for my own good. I am protected from tyrants. It guards me against tension and fragmentation of my self. It anoints me with benefits. Though we pass through hard times, I will be preserved. These strong walls will surely embrace all the days of my life, if I remain a corporation man forever."

Harrington eventually quit the labyrinth of The Palace because he did not want to follow the "clearly defined arrows [that] mark the corporate route that has been laid out for us by our superiors and by the Executive Development Committee." He wanted to follow his own way, rather than play a role and risk ending up like the "wayside zombies who have gone as far as they can go, performing the same duties over and over again."

Harrington was a rare case, even in America. Few workers there abandon the organized life once they have entered it, for their anointed benefits —pay, insurance, pensions, annuities, credit unions, expense accounts and many more—often add up to a private welfare state and they come to depend on it. In other countries, Harrington's defiance would seem stranger than it does in the United States, and in Japan it would probably be considered bizarre. For the aspects of organizational life that Harrington found repellent, the Japanese find attractive.

In Japan, it has been said, a man is known by the company that keeps him. To a degree that many Westerners consider ridiculous—or frightening—the Japanese have transferred their loyalties from their old feudal masters to the large corporations and government bureaucracies of today. And the loyalty flows both ways. Joining a large corporation upon leaving school, the Japanese youth expects to stay with the firm for his entire working life, never to be fired except for criminal acts or on grounds of insanity. In return he is expected to work loyally, to identify with the corporation, to follow the rules and wait his turn—and so he does, with very little of the kind of *angst* that caused Alan Harrington to quit his Crystal Palace. From his corporation the Japanese derives not only livelihood and security, but health care, further education and social life. Every large corporation also has a semiformal system to ensure that the employee's assignments match his personal needs and career desires as much as possible. If he is a young man seeking to marry, the company stands ready to help him find a bride and to provide a priest and a hall for the wedding ceremony. Later he and his family are likely to spend their vacations in the company of fellow employees of the same general rank at mountain or seashore resorts owned and operated by the firm.

That kind of lifelong dependence on a single organization clearly does not fit Western traditions of mobility and diversity. (And in fact there are signs that a new mobility is fraying the Japanese pattern around the edges, too.) It is true that IBM has a company song, that it is still possible to walk along Bond Street in London and see men wearing their old school ties, that at the Watergate hearings in 1973 one young man explained that he committed what he knew were improper acts because of "the fear . . . of not being a team player." But it is unlikely that America or Europe will ever match Japan, where all corporation employees, even lowly broom wielders and delivery boys, proudly wear company emblems in their lapels and announce that "I'm a Mitsubishi man," or "I work for Sony."

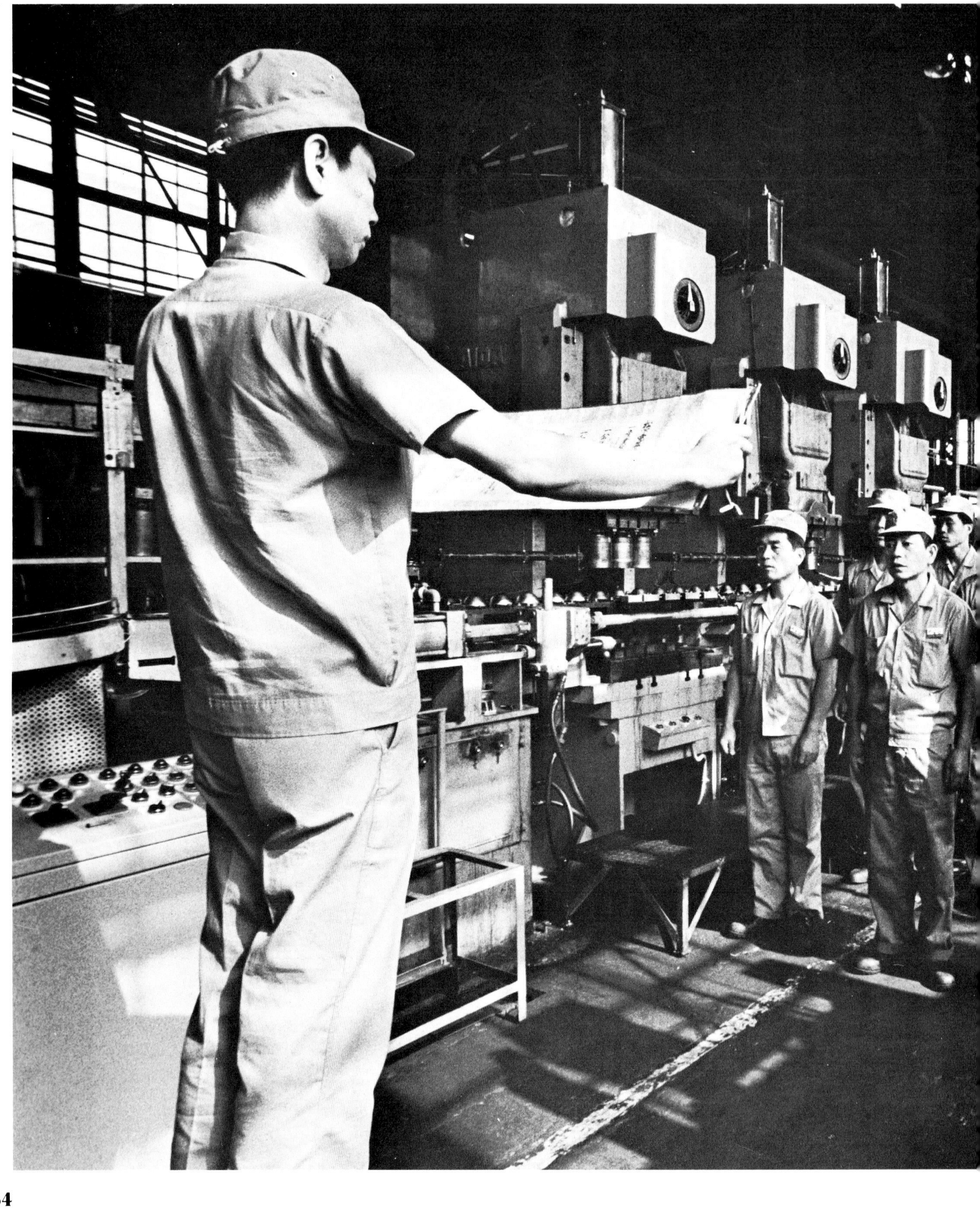

The gung ho company spirit

Probably the most consummately organized men and women in private industry today are the business legions of Japan. There the employer traditionally has been paternalistic toward his workers, and as the companies that struggled into existence after World War II gained international success, the tradition grew ever stronger. In return for employee loyalty, each concern now provides for corporate family womb-to-tomb, anticipating and meeting personal as well as on-the-job needs. The system has significantly blurred the line between a worker's private existence and his organization life.

The most pampered work force is that of the Matsushita Electric Industrial Company, Japan's largest maker of electronic products (Panasonic and other brands). Matsushita has 54,000 employees at its 120 plants throughout the country. From the time anyone is hired, he has job security until he retires at 60. He can be fired only for a crime or insanity. Automation poses no danger; the director of production engineering says, "Our approach is to replace simple jobs with machines and give people more challenging tasks."

The worker is reassured of management's regard for him by twice-yearly cash bonuses of three months' salary, plus a token present on his birthday. Commuters get transportation allowances and everyone, from executives to assembly-line workers, eats low-priced meals at the company's cafeterias. If a worker deposits his money in a Matsushita bank, it earns at three times the usual rate. If his wife becomes pregnant, she can have her baby at a company hospital for about 20 per cent less than the standard fee.

Workers at the Matsushita battery plant in Moriguchi begin their day, standing at attention, by hearing a foreman read the company creed, which includes pledges of diligence, honesty and gratitude. Then they will sing the company song. The ritual is required of all employees, even of the scientists in their laboratories.

Getting out the kinks during their morning break, workers at Matsushita's Moriguchi plant bend and twist in an outdoor session in group calisthenics.

Taking a midafternoon breather, workers exchange assembly-line gossip around the tables in the softly lit, well-appointed lounge of the plant's coffee house.

Male employees end their day with a communal bath before changing into street clothes and going home. The women bathe in an adjoining room.

A break from the tedious round

Many Matsushita workers have jobs that require painstaking accuracy and yet can become monotonous, like soldering a few of the 25,000 different components into a TV chassis moving slowly down an 80-yard-long assembly line. To keep up morale—and efficiency—the company takes pains to make each factory as pleasant physically as possible, and to give employees time during the day to enjoy life.

Every morning and afternoon, the factory work is stopped for 15-minute breaks. For the energetic workers, there are mini tennis courts set up near warehouses. For the less ambitious, there are tree-shaded avenues where an employee can relax on the grass by a roadway until it is time to go back to work.

After hours, more togetherness

At night many Matsushita employees head not for home but for a company gym or classroom. There, at no charge, they pursue a range of activities that the company offers with the aim of reinforcing a sense of group identification. Men learn judo or fencing, women are taught flower arranging and the intricate tea ceremony. Both sexes may study calligraphy, Buddhism, English or Spanish. So popular is the program that, a few years ago, some employees opposed the elimination of Saturday work because they feared consequent weekday overtime might make them late for their classes.

A group of young women employees, most still wearing uniforms the company supplies, spend the evening learning the principles of "ikebana," an ancient and complicated art of flower arrangement.

Members of a Matsushita judo club tussle away workday tensions. The company also has had a punching-bag dummy on factory premises, which employees struck to vent any anger against the bosses.

Under a company slogan urging wisdom, women's teams compete for a volleyball championship. Their shirtmaker, who is presumably not a Matsushita man, has misspelled the name of the concern.

59

This family pays Matsushita $35 a month for a three-room flat, less than half the going rate. They got the company-made TV and refrigerator at a discount.

Wearing a traditional wig and kimono rented from Matsushita, a foreman's new wife cuts into one of the Western-style wedding cakes that are the rage in Japan.

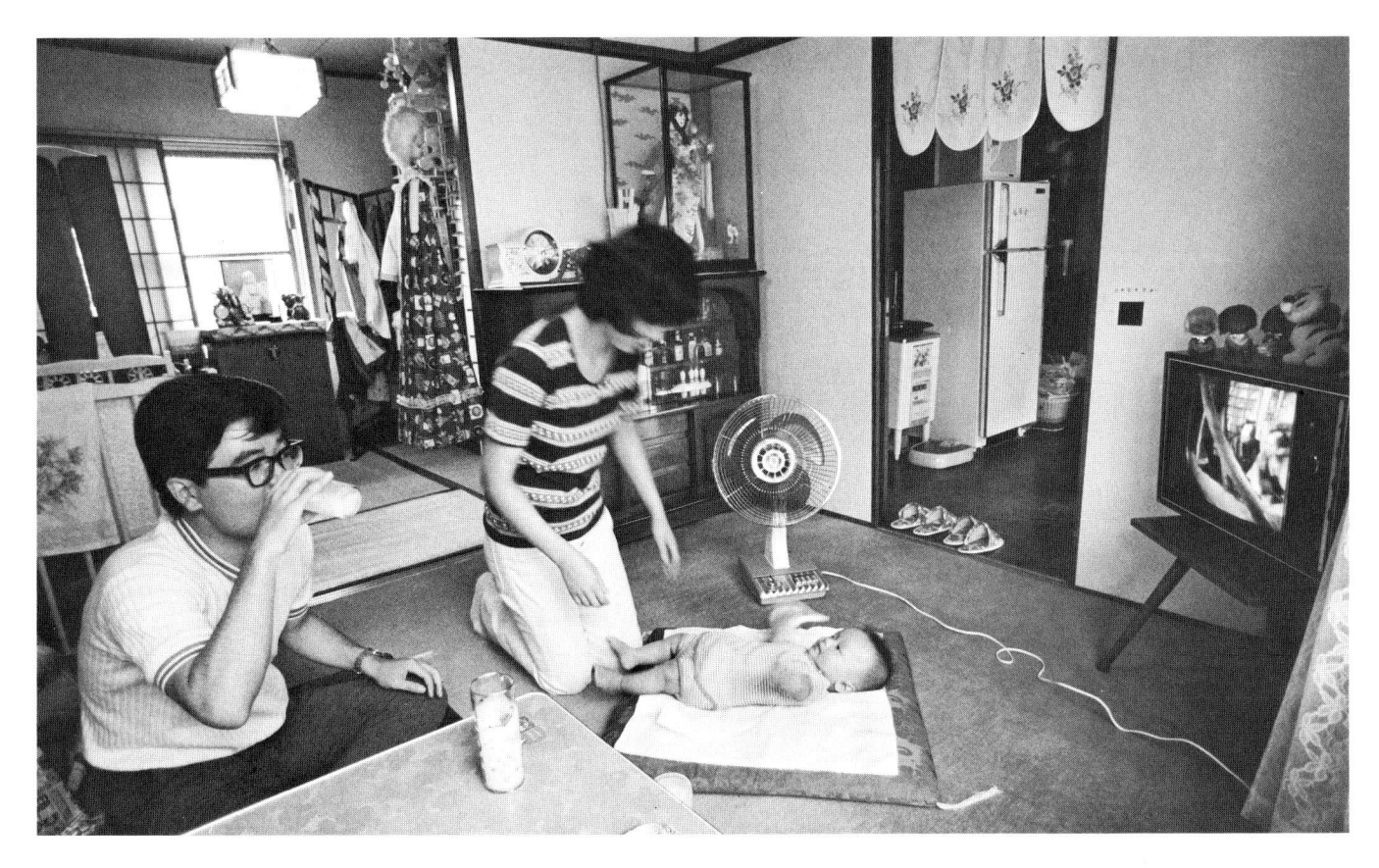

The family plan at Matsushita

If a Matsushita employee wants to marry, a matchmaker in the personnel office will introduce him to a likely mate. If the match works, the couple can be married by a company-hired Shinto priest in a company wedding hall and feted at a company-arranged banquet. The entire cost to the newlyweds is half what it would otherwise be.

The couple can honeymoon at a company hotel *(following pages)*; or if they decide to go abroad, Matsushita's travel bureau will make all arrangements. On their return, they can move into an apartment in one of the 30 company housing projects. When they are ready to build their own home, they can do so on land that the company owns, and finance it with a low-cost company loan.

Budget shopping, two girls appraise kimono materials at one of 60 company stores. The stores sell items from tires to whiskey at a 20 per cent discount.

Flanked by two traditionally landscaped gardens, a couple strolls down the driveway of the nine-acre Senri center for Matsushita workers near Osaka.

Cut-rate vacations at posh retreats

The Japanese anthropologist Chie Nakane has noted that her countrymen tend to think of their factories, and not their residential neighborhoods, as their home villages. So fond are Matsushita workers of their various "villages" that when they go on vacation, they often head for one of the company's 15 recreation centers, to meet fellow villagers from the same plant.

The resorts offer vacation amenities at low rates: a single room is $2.85 a night; dinner costs $1.75 to $3.55. They are in the country, where guests can indulge the Japanese passion for hiking, use miniature golf courses or play table tennis. Mainly, though, there is the chance to socialize with fellow workers. The desire to stay within the corporate community apparently endures for a lifetime—the women at right, meeting at a center for a weekend reunion, all returned to Matsushita after retiring to rear their children.

A vacationer drives a ball across one of the Senri hotel's four tennis courts. Along with a golf driving range and swimming pool, the resort has its own wedding hall.

Some reading and some playing the game go, guests lounge in their communal bedroom at a center in Shokoso. The center provides the women's kimonos free.

62

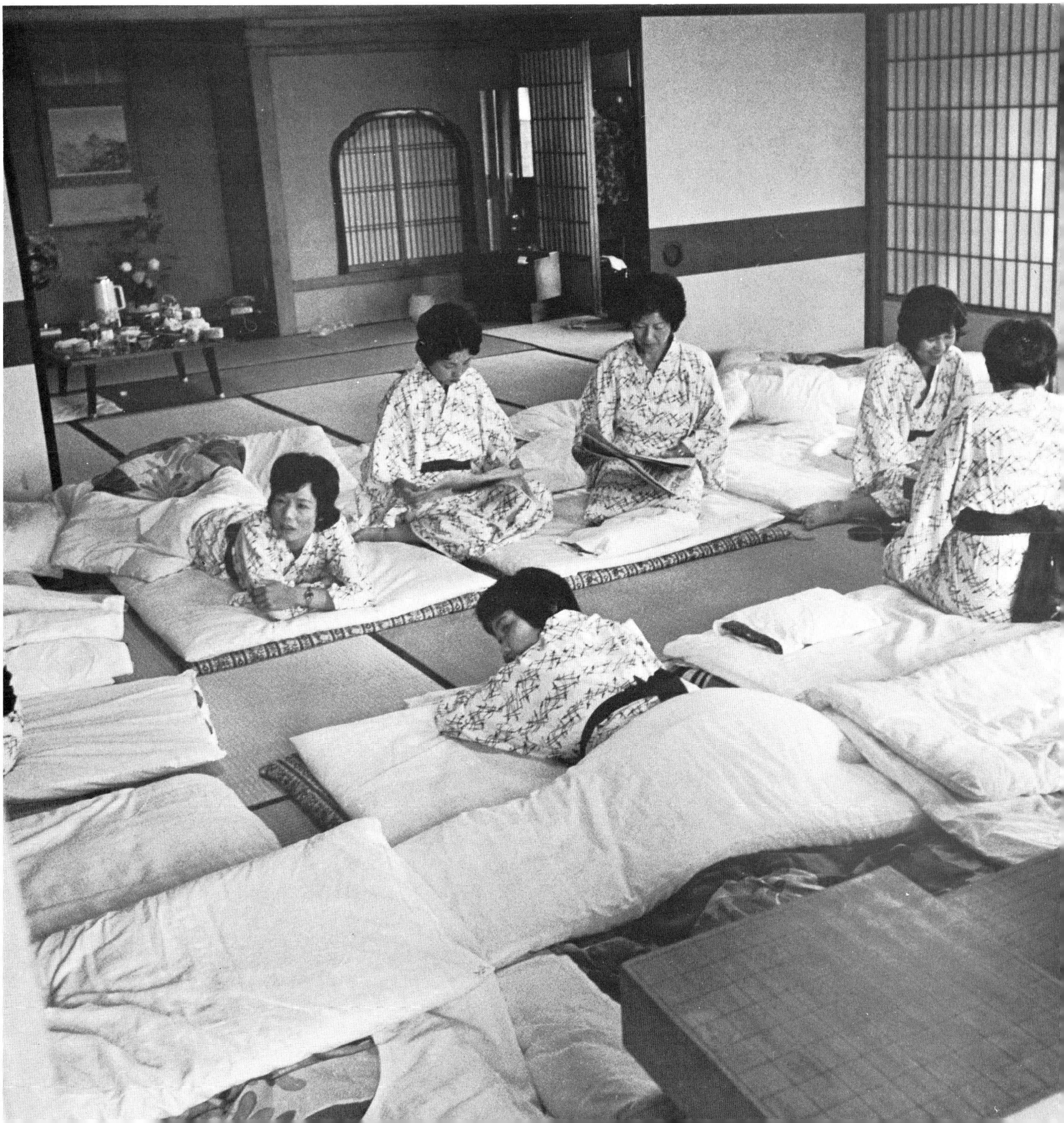

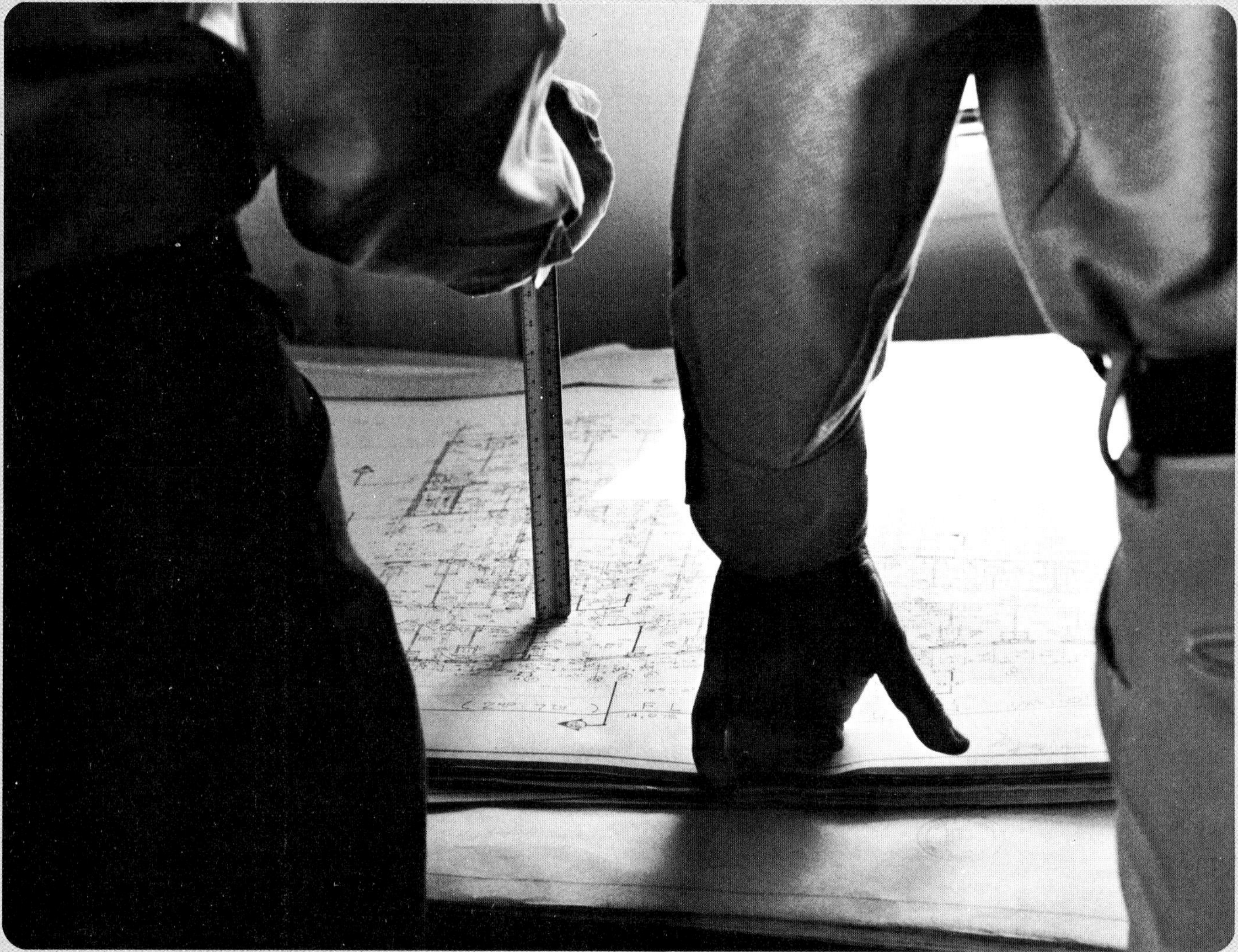

The Formal Structure

Every organization needs a boss, and every boss needs a chain of command. No matter how cooperative and devoted to the organization's mission the individuals within it may be, they cannot be expected to work efficiently together merely by following their own whims and desires. Someone must decide who does what, and to whom, and when. Honest disagreements about the best way to proceed—or about the very purpose of the organization itself—must be settled. Personality conflicts must be neutralized. For the benefit of all, individual preferences must yield to some extent to the needs of the organization—and someone, some *one*—must decide what those needs are. Thus no organization can function unless its members understand where the decision-making authority resides and generally comply with the orders of that authority. There must be a head man and he must be obeyed. For an organization is not a democracy.

A historical case in point is that multinational industrial giant, the General Motors Corporation. In 1919, GM, then a young corporation, was in serious trouble. On the surface it was a fast-growing, successful corporation. In reality, it was suffering from the inflation that followed World War I, a threatening depression—and worst of all, for want of an effective command structure, corporate confusion.

Founded 11 years earlier by William C. Durant, a brilliant, rugged but erratic individualist, GM had burgeoned into a loosely knit, highly decentralized group of 25 different companies. And the thread holding them together was starting to unravel. According to Alfred P. Sloan Jr., then a 43-year-old president of one subsidiary, Durant "was a great man with a great weakness—he could create but not administer." Headquarters executives had lost control of the individual companies; they competed against one another for capital and corporate priorities. They even tried to compete with the flamboyant Durant himself. At one point Walter P. Chrysler collided head-on with Durant about their respective jurisdictions—and lost. He banged the door on the way out, and went on to form the Chrysler Corporation.

Sloan drafted an "Organization Study" proposing "a principle of coordination without losing the advantages of decentralization." Each division would remain autonomous, and its chief would be responsible for its profit. But a separate layer of corporate executives would make overall policy for all divisions; and those people who made policy would be clearly distinguished from those who carried it out. A corporate committee serving as the "federal government" of the decentralized empire would keep track of what each division was doing. It would set priorities for each division and would judge performance not merely on the volume of sales, but on the actual return on invested capital. By the time Sloan finished his organization chart, it contained 116 different little boxes—but the lines of authority from top to bottom were direct and clear.

Durant did nothing about the Sloan memo and chart, probably because they really called for a solid boss like the stolid Sloan. But Durant was soon forced out and by 1923 Sloan was in. His concept—decentralized operations with coordinated central control—certainly worked well for GM. During Sloan's long stewardship the corporation became one of the most successful business enterprises in history, and it has remained so; in 1972 its annual sales totaled more than $30 billion, a figure that maintained General Motors as the largest auto manufacturer in America—and that exceeded the gross national product of all but 15 countries in the world.

Sloan's blueprint became a significant and widely copied working model because it attacked classic problems of the organization in a new way. But it is only one of many variations of a structure that is basic to every large organization, whether an industrial complex, an army or a university. That structure is pyramidal, a hierarchy in which a few people at the apex direct many people at the lower levels. What goes on in the pyramid varies from culture to culture. Sloan's federally controlled decentralization is much applied in the United States but used less in Europe. Yet each of the many methods of directing an organization can work.

Direction means many things: delegation of responsibility, division of labor, setting the long-range goals, giving the day-to-day orders. It also implies the need for compliance. There must be means of exacting performance; depending on the nature of the organization, those means may include voluntary cooperation, money or sheer force. To stay alive and to thrive, the organization also must protect itself from a variety of ills to which it is subject, ranging from fat in the middle to lethal conflicts of authority at the top such as Sloan sought to resolve at GM. All the while, if it is to function efficiently, the organization must have clear channels of communication through which its goals and commands can be transmitted and acknowledged. Finally, but not least, it must keep a sharp eye on its own decision-making process. For whether its decisions are made by executive fiat, by committee or by reasoned consensus, the organization's decisions determine its future, for better or worse.

The general problem of organizing the organization divides into two basic ones: first, deciding what to do, and second, getting everyone to do it. GM's Sloan had no trouble with the first. "Decentralization or not," he said, "an industrial corporation is not the mildest form of organization in a society. I never minimized the administrative power of the chief executive officer in principle when I occupied that position. I simply exercised that power with discretion; I got better results by selling my ideas than by telling people what to do. Yet the power to act must be located in the chief executive officer."

In most organizations, the chief executive is firmly ensconced on top of the pyramid, which is built up of descending layers of power and authority. In theory at least, everyone in the pyramid knows his place; he knows who reports to him, and to whom he reports in turn. Orders flow down, reports flow up, and a chain of command is visibly established.

Not too far from the top, the typical pyramid is divided horizontally into two distinct sections. In the hierarchy of the Roman Catholic Church, for example, the division is between the bishops (including the Pope and the cardinals) and the lesser clergy. Only the bishops carry the "fullness of the priesthood," the power to ordain new priests. Because the Church holds that its authority stems in direct succession from the apostles, who in turn received it from Christ, the right to carry on that succession by ordaining new priests is crucial to the survival of the institution.

In modern military organizations, a similar line is drawn between officers and enlisted men. Commissioned officers receive their appointments from a higher authority (from the Congress in America, the sovereign in England, the president in France). In the United States, only a commissioned officer can swear in new recruits, promote an enlisted man or mete out formal punishment. The commissioned officer thus carries the same fullness in his profession as the bishop does in his.

In private organizations, management and workers form the two distinct classes within the pyramid. Management makes the policy decisions, hires and fires, and carries a fullness to the extent that its members are supposed to believe in and identify with the organization. Workers, on the other hand, generally make only immediate day-by-day technical decisions on their specific jobs; they have to be motivated to do their jobs—or so the theory goes—and often are not expected to show the same fullness of loyalty to the organization.

The mantle of fullness generally confers on its wearer the authority to issue orders. But many members of organizations—priests and bishops, noncoms and officers, foremen and management—give some orders. And they obey some. That is the purpose of the pyramid. Why it works so well has been the subject of much study. One sophisticated analysis of the operation of organizational authority has been developed by Columbia University sociologist Amitai Etzioni. He classifies organizations into three categories—coercive, normative and utilitarian—based on what he calls their "nature of compliance." People obey orders, Etzioni says, because they are forced to (in coercive organizations), because they want to, for voluntary moral or social reasons (in normative organizations), or because they get paid to (in utilitarian organizations).

Etzioni lists two notoriously coercive organizations—prisons and custodial mental hospitals—but similar coercive types include concentration camps, correctional institutions, POW camps and relocation centers. They all exercise control by the use of force, and their "members" are without doubt alienated from the organizations.

Pure coercion alone, however, does not work in other types of organizations. As Rousseau explained, "The strongest is never strong enough to be always the master unless he transforms might into right and obedience into duty." Such a transformation—of obedience into duty—occurs in normative organizations. Members of such structures are highly committed to the organization's goals; therefore they can be controlled by threats of expulsion or by ostracism, or by the granting or withholding of status symbols. Religious organizations, political parties, hospital medical staffs, professional and fraternal associations, and colleges and universities by that definition are all normative.

Etzioni's third category—utilitarian organizations—exacts obedience by paying for it, and the members obey in order to get paid. They are neither highly committed nor completely alienated; they identify with the or-

Originator of a widely used plan for allocating authority within large American corporations, Alfred P. Sloan Jr. addresses General Motors workmen in 1937. Sloan structured GM, centralizing policy control so as to ride herd on its autonomously operated divisions.

ganization only so long as they regard their employment as a fair deal. Most levels of most industries fall into this category.

Few organizations of any type rely entirely on one kind of authority. Corporations may be basically utilitarian but their managers and white-collar employees can be manipulated or disciplined by normative means, such as the conferring of status symbols or the application of incentives. Etzioni cites one study of what he calls "non-remunerative symbolic controls" used on one white-collar group. Salesgirls who made mistakes in writing out sales slips were reprimanded by holding them up to shame. The offending girls got their unacceptable slips back—marked with a telltale, red rubber band. They then had to correct the slips in the presence of their colleagues, broadcasting the disgrace.

Some organizations use all three systems of compliance, although not simultaneously. In peacetime a volunteer army is primarily utilitarian. Some soldiers may enlist for patriotic reasons but more of them probably sign up for the pay, to see the world or to get an education. But the compliance system shifts drastically when the guns start firing. No army could pay its soldiers enough to compensate for the risks and hardships of war; troops must be motivated by other methods. The first, normative: prayers, appeals to patriotism, indoctrination designed to convince the soldier that his sacrifice is vital to some higher purpose. If that fails, the army then turns to coercion, court-martialing deserters and threatening to shoot men who turn and run from battle.

The three different kinds of organizations respond to different applications of rules and regulations. Formal bureaucratic rules, naturally, tend to be more effective in utilitarian organizations than in normative ones. A few years ago a study was done of a container-manufacturing corporation in Ohio, comparing the rules, structures, supervision, controls and delegation of responsibility of two of its automated plants and two research laboratories. One plant and one laboratory were highly efficient; the others were not. The findings were unequivocal. The efficient plant "had a pattern of formal relationships and duties that was highly structured and precisely defined." One manager told the researchers, "We make sure each man knows his job, knows when he can take a break, knows how to handle a change of shifts. It's all spelled out clearly for him the day he comes to work here." Another added: "We've got rules here for everything from how much powder to use in cleaning the toilet bowls to how to cart a dead body out of the plant." The less efficient plant, on the other hand, was much less carefully structured. It had fewer precise rules, more lower-level participation in decision making and a more "egalitarian distribution of influence."

The findings for the two laboratories, however, were exactly the opposite. The successful one had few formal rules—and they were loosely carried out. Scientists felt free to choose their own tasks and procedures, and they all participated in a wide range of decisions; they rarely felt control from above. "If a man puts a nut on a screw all day long," one scientist said, "you may need more rules and a job definition for him. But we're professionals and not the kind who need close supervision." In the less successful lab, all decisions were made at the top. Scientists there felt restricted by rules and formal duties and complained that the lab was not properly utilizing their expertise. Said one employee: "It's hard to put your finger on, but I guess I'd call it 'Mickey Mouse.' There are rules and things here that get in your way."

The authors of the study concluded, sensibly enough, that the best pattern of organization depends "on the nature of the work to be done"—but they added, significantly, "and on the particular needs of the people involved." The repetitive tasks of utilitarian factories, unless imaginatively organized, may call for highly specific procedures and classical management hierarchies. Normative scientists, faced with unpredictable and changing research tasks that require more extensive problem solving, would be expected to work better in an informal atmosphere that allows them a chance to make decisions on their own. But the needs of the people involved may turn those conclusions topsy-turvy, making strict authoritarianism self-defeating on some assembly lines *(Chapter 6)* and useful in some laboratories.

The conflicting demands of work and people often lead to clashes. The extreme example is the large hospital, where several types of authority —normative, utilitarian and even coercive—are pressed to their limits. The medical personnel usually are normative, inspired by the ideals of their profession and working within considerations of status, prestige and ethics; they regard the hospital as a service institution. The nonmedical, utilitarian administrators, on the other hand, must be concerned with the day-to-day business of whether the hospital stays within its budget. And for some patients, authority is coercive.

Professor of sociology Harvey L. Smith of the University of North Carolina found one large hospital where the medical director—a physician —was ready to resign because his supervisor was a layman who, according to the doctor, just "did not know enough" about medical problems to run a hospital. The unhappy physician was also in a dilemma about his own status because he had two hats to wear—was he a doctor or an administrator? At another hospital in the study, the rivalry between two administrators —one trained as a nurse and the other as a businessman—became so intense that two separate organization charts had to be drafted. The chart shown to the public displayed the humanitarian nurse-administrator as the boss; the chart shown to the trustees, however, listed the business manager as the top executive.

Another source of conflict in many organizations is created by a substructure characteristic of nearly all pyramidal hierarchies: the distinction between "line" officers, who supervise the principal work of the organization, and "staff" experts of various kinds who supply them with information and advice or perform specialized tasks.

In the U.S. Army, for example, every unit larger than a company has

continued on page 75

For the deeply religious monks of Casamari, Italy, every day begins at 3:45 a.m. Obedient to abbey rules, they arise in darkness and in silent procession wend their way through vaulted halls to their Gothic basilica for prayers.

The regimented religious life

For almost a thousand years in Casamari, Italy, not far from Rome, an austere monastic order has survived —even though it exacts the utmost in personal sacrifice from its members. The order is a pure example of what sociologists call a normative organization, whose members follow its regulations simply because they believe in them. In this case the motive is faith in God: The 70-odd Cistercian monks at Casamari, along with their counterparts in similar orders elsewhere, believe they can save their souls by forsaking the world and subordinating themselves to their religious organization.

Every Cistercian vows obedience to the Rule of St. Benedict, a detailed set of precepts for daily life drawn up by Benedict of Nursia in the Sixth Century. In conformity with the Rule, each believer remains for life in the order. Each embraces chastity throughout life, silence through most of the day and everlasting poverty. "Let no one presume to have anything as his own, anything whatever," Benedict wrote. And because Benedict's followers agree with his assertion that "idleness is the enemy of the soul," they devote eight hours a day to religious observances and another six hours to work.

71

Cistercian monks sing morning prayers according to the ritual prescribed by their order.

Hour by hour through a long day

As members of a voluntary organization, the monks of Casamari follow a routine that outsiders uncommitted to Cistercian ideals would find unendurably oppressive. The day's *horarium*, or schedule, outlined below begins at 3:45 a.m. and ends at 8:45 p.m., fulfilling the precepts of austerity laid down by St. Benedict in the Middle Ages.

3:45 a.m. The day begins.

4:00 a.m. Prayers in the basilica.

5:00 a.m. Optional Mass.

6:30 a.m. Readings from St. Benedict's Rule.

6:45 a.m. Meditation in the basilica.

7:00 a.m. Choral Mass.

8:00 a.m. Breakfast in the refectory.

9:00 a.m. Work period—study, teaching or manual labor.

12:15 p.m. Prayers in the basilica.

12:30 p.m. Lunch, as portions of the Bible are read aloud.

1:30 p.m. Free period.

2:15 p.m. Vespers in the basilica.

2:45 p.m. Work.

6:20 p.m. Meditation and prayer.

7:00 p.m. Supper.

7:30 p.m. Thanksgiving service.

7:45 p.m. Free period.

8:15 p.m. Readings from religious works or biographies.

8:30 p.m. Final prayers.

8:45 p.m. Monks retire to their cells.

This aspirant, whose black hood shows he has taken preliminary vows, studies in his cell to become a full-fledged monk.

To support their organization, monks distill liqueurs to sell. Herbs for flavoring (bowl at left) are crushed with a press (center) and ground in a mortar (right).

At the refectory table for luncheon, the monks forgo chatting, as required by abbey regulations. On religious holidays mealtime conversation is permitted.

73

As each regimented day ends, the abbot who heads the monastery at Casamari blesses the monks as they file past him before retiring.

four principal staff sections: S-1 is personnel and training, S-2 is intelligence, S-3 operations and planning, and S-4 logistics and supply. (If the unit is big enough to be commanded by a general, these sections are called G-1, G-2 and so on.) Every staff officer takes orders from the commander of his unit, but he is linked to higher and lower echelons of his staff specialty as well. Among other advantages, this arrangement provides several channels of communication to backstop the primary chain of command. When the staffs are functioning properly, every commander will get the information he needs—and should he do something unwise his superiors are likely to hear about it through the staff network in time to take the appropriate action.

When the Army was younger and simpler, junior officers rotated through staff and line positions until those with the ability "to lead men" could be selected for higher command, while the others sought congenial staff careers. Traditionally the line has been the quickest route to military promotion and glory; line officers still tend to look down on staff officers, who find solace and status in their specialized knowledge and expertise. Nowadays, as the military establishment grows more complex, with automated weapons, specialized staff schools and sophisticated auditing and control techniques borrowed from business management, the distinction between line and staff becomes even more pronounced.

In most corporations this distinction is regarded as that of "doers" versus "thinkers." Authority to see that the main job gets done is delegated to the line personnel because they have demonstrated—often in on-the-job activity—an exceptional ability to command; the staff man's authority comes from his own professional expertise and standing—in engineering, accounting or some other specialty. The loyalties of staff men are frequently questioned because their allegiance is to what they regard as the purer values and norms of their professions. If they have more formal education, as often is the case, they may look down upon line officials, who, in turn, tend to regard their staff colleagues as impractical dreamers unaware of the realities of organizational life.

Mutual antagonism often arises out of these differing attitudes and systems of loyalty. One factory foreman described an engineer as "a guy who comes around and picks your brain on the fine points of the job, then goes to your boss and gets his approval to come back in two weeks and tell you how to do your job." From the other side, an engineer at the same factory spoke of his frustration: "We're always in hot water with these old guys in the line. You can't tell them a damn thing. They're bull-headed as hell. Most of the time we offer a suggestion it's either laughed at or not considered at all. The same idea in the mouth of some old codger in the line would get a round of applause. They treat us like kids."

For all the conflicts between line and staff—and the antagonisms are probably inevitable—the line-staff concept does enable people of widely disparate experience, attitudes and skills to work together for a common goal. It serves this purpose partly by its division of authority within the pyramid—decisions on what is to be done are made by the line, decisions on how it may best be accomplished depend heavily on the staff.

The line-staff division is only one way in which authority is split up; some division is obviously necessary because no individual can effectively supervise too large a number of subordinates. The number he can supervise is known as his span of control, and it varies greatly according to the type of work being carried out. When the work is routine, or when many subordinates are performing similar jobs, the span of control is fairly broad; when closer supervision is necessary, the span of control is correspondingly narrowed. A factory foreman might be able to supervise 30 or more men on an assembly line, while a corporation president might insist, as Sloan properly did, that he directly oversee only a handful of other top executives.

This built-in limitation on an individual's span of control helps explain

Inside a cell block of Mexico City's notorious Lecumberri Prison—the Black Palace—inmates line up as ordered for noon roll call. Like others who are incarcerated, these prisoners are, involuntarily, members of the kind of organization classed as coercive—its roles and behavior are controlled by force.

why the pyramids of many organizations get to be top-heavy as they grow larger. Ten men doing a job may need only one boss; 20 men require not only one more boss, but also a new supervisor for the two bosses. As the organization continues to expand, it adds supervisors at an even faster rate. Today some large corporations—such as British Airways and Mitsubishi—have as many as 15 or 20 clearly defined echelons within their pyramids, and feel they need them.

It is conceivable that at least part of the manpower added on by growth may result from "bureaucratic bloat," an organizational disease described in the wryly humorous—but astonishingly perceptive—book *Parkinson's Law* by C. Northcote Parkinson. A British professor who had written many scholarly books on history and politics, Parkinson worked during World War II for the British War Office and the Royal Air Force, and during this service formulated Parkinson's Law: "Work expands so as to fill the time available for its completion." The corollary to Parkinson's Law was also stated: "There need be little or no relationship between the work to be done and the size of the staff."

Parkinson calculated that the number of subordinates in any organization multiplies at an annual rate of between 5.17 and 6.56 per cent, even when output actually decreases. He considered the British Admiralty the classic illustration of his law. It had grown from 2,000 to 3,569 officials during a period in which the Royal Navy's uniformed manpower decreased by one third and the number of ships decreased by two thirds. The gold braid "would have multiplied at the same rate had there been no actual seamen at all," Parkinson said.

Bureaucratic officialdom everywhere—not just in the British Admiralty—does proliferate, and it is often difficult to determine how much of the growth is bloat, or how much is justifiable growth. A study of the New York City Police Department in 1974 revealed that the force had grown by 55 per cent over the previous 20 years, while the number of policemen walking a beat or cruising in patrol cars had remained about the same. In 1973, Italy had almost 60,000 different tax-supported agencies, each with a salaried president; one out of every 900 Italians was a president of some kind of public organization. That same year Italy had more admirals than ships in its Navy, and one general for every 5,000 troops in the Army, compared to a United States ratio of one general for every 20,000 troops. The French ratio was even more Parkinsonian than the Italian, and might even put the British Admiralty to shame: one general or admiral for every 1,700 men!

In the Soviet Union, where central state organizations control most industrial and governmental activities, the top-heavy bureaucracy is a favorite target of humor. Indeed, the leading Soviet comedian, Arkady Raikin, performs a popular and devastating routine in which he exemplifies bureaucratic bloat at its purest. He plays the role of a minor official who one day at the office literally loses his head, and hardly misses it. Neither do his visitors. His secretary notices nothing amiss. The official realizes that his job is so useless the state would be better off if he never went to work at all.

Another book that is meant to amuse while revealing some fundamental truths about how large organizations, and the people in them, frequently behave is *The Peter Principle*, by a California education professor, Laurence J. Peter.

The Peter Principle bluntly reveals how people advance in institutional bureaucracies. "In a hierarchy every employee tends to rise to his level of incompetence." That is, people who do their work well tend to get promoted until they finally land a job too difficult for them. At that point they stop getting promotions, which leads to Peter's Corollary: "In time, every post tends to be occupied by an employee who is incompetent to carry out his duties." Thus, according to Peter, real work in an organization is performed only by those who have not yet reached their "final placement" of incompetence.

Commenting on the Peter Principle in the *Harvard Business Review*, one professor of management suggested that organizations are still able to function—despite the incompetents—because women and other suppressed minorities, such as blacks and immigrants, are not permitted to rise to positions they cannot handle; they remain instead in jobs they can perform efficiently. But the real flaw in the Peter Principle is probably simpler: Most employees are not promoted high enough to test their mettle. If six equally competent individuals are working in a department, and one

A wedding knot tied in red tape

The red tape spawned by organizational rules so entangles government agencies that President John F. Kennedy once likened dealing with them to trying to nail jelly to the wall. He was talking about the American bureaucracy, but among the more notorious examples of a nation trapped in paper work is Italy.

The experience of the Roman couple at right—Cinzia, an 18-year-old secretary, and Italo, 25, a bank employee—can only be called routine for Italy. When they decided on a wedding date, they scheduled their vacations for the same time and stayed in the city just so they could get all the necessary civil and church permits. They encountered no unusual delays. Nevertheless the process took them six full weeks.

Starting out at the city registry in Rome, Cinzia and Italo obtain forms requesting special birth certificates and papers verifying their residences.

of them is promoted over the others to his final level of incompetence, five competent people remain to do the job. And there they probably stay, for their newly incompetent boss is not likely to get any further promotions to make room for them.

The Peter Principle and Parkinson's Law most seriously affect the upper levels of organizations. This susceptibility of the higher echelons is understandable. Clearly it is difficult to find people competent for the most difficult jobs, the ones demanding superior abilities, and an incompetent is often selected simply because he is the best available. When his inability to handle the job is recognized, the common remedy is the addition of more employees who are expected to produce enough to make up for the incompetent's deficiencies.

Although this process affects all the operations of an organization, influence on the most important task of all—decision making—may be considerable. Decisions must be made—and made quickly, firmly and clearly. The decision itself may turn out to be right or wrong, but if it is not made at all, the organizational pyramid is likely to become just another ancient monument.

Who makes the decision is often less important than guaranteeing that one is made. In fact, what the decision is may not be crucial—so long as decisive action is taken. Since flawless solutions rarely present themselves, perfectionists are likely to hem and haw themselves into a disaster. An indecisive manager usually finds that a more confident colleague has made

Filling out forms to get the papers, they confront the 12 separate parts of the applications for their birth certificates.

Paying in advance for the birth certificates, Cinzia and Italo line up at a cashier's window. They will leave their requests for the certificates with the clerk.

continued

Chapter 3

the decision for him—and has, not incidentally, taken the first step toward easing him out of a job. Confidence, or even the appearance of confidence, is often the key to advancement. As one successful executive at a television network puts it: "Many times it doesn't matter what you decide, as long as you decide, because either course will turn out okay as long as everybody pitches in and works for it. So even if you're not one hundred per cent sure, the trick is to act as if you are."

Such confidence, of course, can be catching—and that can be dangerous. If members of a decision-making group happen to share the same basic values, if they attach more importance to the approval of their colleagues than to solving the problem, if they want to "get ahead," then the process of decision making can become mere "groupthink," a treacherous aberration.

Groupthink is committee management at its worst—decisions made out of a need to conform, to go along with accepted ideas and avoid dispute. It tends to take over when a cozy atmosphere, mutual loyalty and team spirit are so valuable to the members that they readily agree with each other, thereby failing to examine all sides of the problem before them. In such an atmosphere, questioning another member too closely can violate unspoken norms; openly disagreeing may even be considered a personal attack on the leader and the values of the group. Doubters, therefore, remain silent; their silence is taken for assent and each person's assent reinforces every other member's confidence in the wisdom of the com-

Wedding red tape *continued*

Completing requests for residence certificates, Cinzia copies an identification card and Italo uses his driver's license.

Getting their residence certificates, Italo waits with Cinzia at the alphabetical window for her surname, which is Carosi.

Returning to the registry office after a week's wait, Cinzia and Italo find their prepaid birth certificates waiting.

posite thinking. The group may cling together even more solidly in times of crisis—which is just when sharp, independent and even divergent judgments are needed most.

Decades ago, General Motors' Alfred Sloan was aware of the perils of groupthink. He once told a meeting of his policy makers: "Gentlemen, I take it we are all in complete agreement on the decision here. Then I propose we postpone further discussion until our next meeting to give ourselves time to develop disagreement and perhaps gain some understanding of what the decision is all about." The ancient Persians had a more direct way of bringing out divergent opinions: Whenever their generals had decided some important matter, they would deliberately get drunk and consider it again, the theory being that wine would let them speak more freely, without sober inhibition. History has not recorded the effect of such libations on their decisions.

In America there have been two gruesome modern examples of groupthink in action—Pearl Harbor and The Bay of Pigs. Before the Japanese attack on Pearl Harbor, the U.S. Navy knew that Japanese aircraft carriers were operating in the Pacific, but had no idea where the carriers were heading. To the Navy commander in the area, the notion that the Japanese might be on their way to attack his impregnable base was so outlandish that he openly made jokes about it, thus signaling to his ingroup of fellow officers that it was a laughing matter. In that mood of clubby geniality no officer dared risk ridicule by recommending even minimum

Presenting the certificates plus some church records for herself and Italo to her priest, Cinzia and her father get a request for civil banns.

Submitting the banns request at the city registry, the couple is given a date on which they must swear a civil oath.

continued

protective steps, such as sending reconnaissance planes to search the ocean for the Japanese fleet.

Two decades later, when the CIA's plan to invade Cuba came before President John F. Kennedy's advisors, they failed to subject it to the searching examination it obviously needed. Flushed with their electoral victory, convinced of the inherent morality and rightness of their in-group, they felt invulnerable. They neglected to demand a full range of alternatives and dismissed opposing views simply because the critics were outsiders. When one close advisor did express doubts, Robert Kennedy took him aside and said: "You may be right or you may be wrong, but the President has made up his mind. Don't push it any further. Now is the time for everyone to help him all they can."

Groupthink should not be confused with decision by consensus, a peculiarly Japanese approach to decision making. Consensus begins by defining what the problem is; only when all the people involved have agreed on the identity of the problem and on the need to make a decision do specific solutions begin to emerge. Rooted in pragmatism, Japanese-style consensus assumes that no view is necessarily good or bad. Instead of riding roughshod over a minority view, the Japanese seek a solution with which everyone can go along. Since everyone involved in the process knows that his views will be reflected somehow in the final decision, and that he will not be considered disloyal or evil or crazy for holding them, he will speak up, even if he is questioning the very fundamentals of earlier pol-

Wedding red tape *continued*

Signing an oath that will permit the posting of religious banns, Italo is directed by Cinzia's priest. She and the couple's parents must also take the oath.

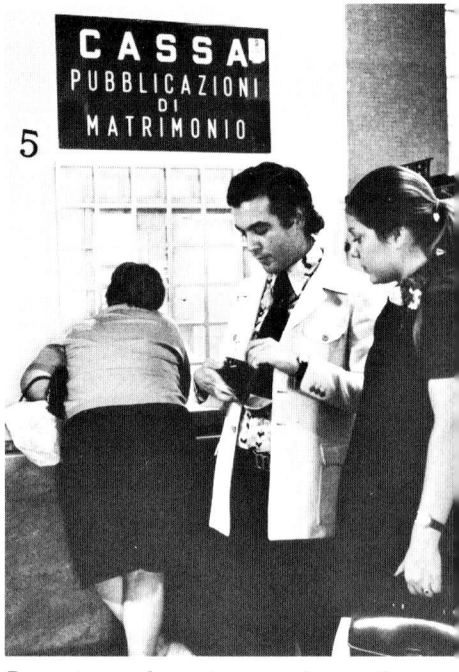

Returning to the registry to take a civil oath—which is also a formal request for civil banns—the pair pays the fee.

icy. That policy, after all, was his as well and in questioning it he does not automatically criticize the wisdom of someone else.

By and large, this system prevents policy disagreements from becoming tangled in power struggles between factions. It also gives all possible alternative courses of action a fair hearing and enables the Japanese to reverse themselves abruptly when conditions warrant. In 1969, for example, only three years after they had decided not to expand internationally, several large Japanese firms were flexible enough to change their minds, make a smooth 180-degree turnabout and begin establishing overseas subsidiaries.

Once a decision is made, efficient communications are necessary to carry it out. Communication down the pyramid starts with broad policies and directives that must be fleshed out with detailed instructions all along the line. Upward communication, including confirmation that the downward message got through in the first place as well as progress reports on what happened later, must be filtered, condensed and integrated; otherwise, executives might be inundated by more detail than they can digest. This is the reason for "going through channels": At each relay point someone must decide what questions and information should—or should not—be bucked on to the next level of authority.

No matter how an organization chooses to systematize the flow of its communications from the top down—memoranda, mass meetings, bulletin boards, employee handbooks—the system must also provide for "feed-

Signing the civil oath, Cinzia's mother writes her name on the paper, which already has been signed by the engaged couple and Italo's father.

Admiring the civil banns, Cinzia and Italo still have 17 days to wait for one more certificate they need to marry.

back," communication from the bottom up. Recent studies of 14 general hospitals in England showed how important feedback is. In hospitals where information flowed in a continuous circle from staff down to student nurses down to patients and back up again, there was a lower turnover rate among the student nurses—and patients seemed to recover faster—than in hospitals where feedback was discouraged and information flowed in only one direction, from the top down.

In some organizations communication is an awesomely extensive process. At the W. R. Grace Corporation, a steamship line that turned itself into a large conglomerate, executives who traveled widely in Latin America on company business in the 1950s were required to write "trip letters" every day, reporting fully on everything they observed. If two Grace executives traveled together, both of them wrote daily letters, exchanged copies and sent them back to headquarters where they were routed to everyone remotely concerned with the contents.

The volume of detailed correspondence that every Grace executive was expected to read was remarkable. Each member of a six-man executive committee received copies of all incoming and outgoing cables and teletypes—sometimes as many as 250 a day—as well as dozens of letters or

Organizational protocol has fouled up the situation so much more than normally for this South Korean naval officer that he breaks down and cries on the parade ground. Forced by regulations to keep his men standing in the sun for hours, awaiting an unaccountably delayed dignitary, he sobs in sheer frustration.

memos. This deluge of information was meant to serve an important purpose. Even the president of the Grace steamship division—if he chose to wade through the flood of paper—could be informed promptly about, say, trouble with a boiler in a sugar refinery in Peru. If all the other executives happened to be away, he could cope with the problem. This practice may have produced some benefits of "executive interchangeability," but Grace finally gave it up when the mountains of paper work produced by its executives became too cumbersome.

Other forms of internal communication can be even more difficult. Communicating with the boss, in fact, can be a delicate exercise in psychology. Messengers who bring bad tidings no longer lose their heads, as they sometimes did in the past, but they do run the risk of exposing themselves to the anger of their superiors, who may forever after remember them only in connection with disaster. On the other hand, yes men who dare not contradict the boss or bring up sticky problems may be feeding his ego, but at the same time they are starving his brain of the information he needs to do his job. And they certainly deprive him of alternatives.

One executive who was determined to promote honest communications with his staff was Alan Boyd, who became president of the Illinois Central Railroad in 1969. The company was, he recalls, "a typical Army operation, 'yes sir,' 'no sir,' 'no excuse, sir' and any time you asked a question you were going to get an answer whether the individual had any idea what he was talking about or not."

Boyd tried to loosen things up by launching an "open-door policy," encouraging his subordinates to come in at any time to talk about whatever was on their minds. They were hesitant, however, and Boyd made slow progress until one day he and a vice president got into an argument in front of other top executives. "We had a real Donnybrook," Boyd says. "This was the first time that a lot of these people had seen us put our act on. It wasn't an act. He and I were really mad, but not at each other. We just had very strong different views. As a result of that altercation, a number of those other fellows are now willing to talk to me and to say, 'Now look, boss, this won't work.' "

At IBM the open-door scheme was first proclaimed as official management policy by Thomas J. Watson Sr., and the company insists that its executives on every level still make use of it. Watson opened his door to allow all his employees to carry their personal grievances to high authority. Used that way, as a means of settling personnel complaints, the open door can be effective because it minimizes the chance that a just grievance will be suppressed by an unsympathetic underling. But it brings its own problems. Ari Kiev, a New York Hospital-Cornell Medical Center expert on executive behavior, has pointed out that employees may actually resent the open door because it implies the boss is an agreeable fellow, whereas he may really be disagreeably terrible-tempered. In such cases the employees know that the boss really does not want them barging in on him all the time, and they are not likely to risk bringing bad news or raising disturbing issues unless they absolutely have to. No matter how wide open the boss's door is, Kiev believes, "the information coming in is likely to be the kind people think he wants to receive."

If the executive keeps his door closed—as most do—he must post a gatekeeper to guard it. The gatekeeper's prime function is to preserve the privacy the executive needs to concentrate on his work. But another, more subtle game is in progress as well. The gatekeepers are protecting the executive's role and image by keeping out people whom he might have to treat harshly or heartlessly—a subordinate who has blundered, for instance, or a petitioner whose case is hopeless. But whether they are receptionists dealing with clients and the public, or secretaries fending off the urgent pleas of other members of the staff, the gatekeepers are in a position to amass more discretionary power than either their bosses intended or their own rank and qualifications deserve.

Many bosses set up these barriers as an elaborate status symbol. "Look at me," they seem to be saying, "I am so busy, and my work is so important, that I cannot waste my time with your trifles." In a sense their gatekeepers replace the pomp and ritual of old royal courts, or the high, distant balcony on which the Pope is seen by the faithful, enveloping the great personage in a fog of awe. When two of these nabobs wish to talk to each other on the telephone, all the gatekeeper's skills are mobilized for the duel. Each secretary strives artfully to maneuver the other one's boss to pick up the telephone first. For some reason it is a loss of face for Mr. Big to pick up his phone and say "Hello, Harry," only to hear Harry's triumphant secretary tell him to hang on because "Mr. Bigger will be on the line in a moment, sir."

Gatekeeper power reached a zenith in President Richard Nixon's administration when Cabinet officers, four-star generals, state governors and captains of industry who wanted to see the President had to deal with a previously obscure advertising executive with no government experience. As the President's gatekeeper, H. R. Haldeman screened what the visitors intended to say and decided whether to admit them according to his views of what Mr. Nixon wanted to hear. Officially, of course, he was merely following the President's orders, but the President often had no means of knowing what was on the mind of the man requesting an audience except as Haldeman chose to interpret it.

Haldeman may have imported his style of gatekeeping with him directly from the Los Angeles advertising agency where he had previously worked. According to a former colleague of his, every top executive of that agency was "surrounded by a tight inner guard of terribly efficient second-banana types who were happy to work in the shadow of a great man. Their function was to protect their leader from surprises. When you would ask to see one of these cossetted executives you had to reveal what you wanted to say to him and precisely how you planned to say it, and any hostile word or tone would mean you wouldn't get in. Everything had to be predictable. And that wasn't true at any other agency that I have ever worked for."

If an open door or a gatekeeper does not bring the boss all the information he needs, neither does any other single method of communication. A variety of channels are kept open by the successful organization, for the information that flows up and down is what helps it adapt to changing circumstances. It cannot remain static, for pressures from within and without continually force it to adjust its shape. There have been many new organizational shapes since thousands upon thousands of laborers and specialists were organized by the Pharaohs to build pyramids and the Chinese to build the Great Wall.

From the time the Industrial Revolution began to bring most of human civilization within the ranks of one organization or another, at least three identifiable generations of organizational structure have appeared. The first, relatively simple one—personal management by the oldtime entrepreneurs and their families—gave way, as organizations became more complex, to Alfred P. Sloan's federal decentralization. That was designed basically for a one-product, one-market operation, and it in turn evolved into the more complex structures required to make modern, multinational, highly diversified corporations work.

No one has all the answers yet for the fourth-generation structures. Organizational theory is changing so fast that theorizing itself has become a growth industry. But some trends are noticeable. Private and public organizations increasingly turn to "task-force management": specialists plucked from permanent positions and grouped into teams to handle specific, short-range projects. This approach was pioneered in the mammoth —and spectacularly successful—effort to land human explorers on the moon *(pages 88-99)*. It brings many unique advantages. Bureaucratic bloat is less of a danger, regular rank and status can be ignored and divisional conflict forgotten because the team is temporary and each member knows he will return to his regular position when the task at hand has been accomplished.

Some organizational theorists now even question the basic, age-old concept of pyramidal, vertical hierarchy. Alvin Toffler predicts in his book *Future Shock*, for example, that automation eventually will do away with the need for bureaucratic organizations. When that happens, his theory goes, personal relationships within the organization will become more important than bureaucratic authority. Some experts predict that organizations with "horizontal" structures, or with no formal structure at all, will better fulfill the needs of the individuals within them. So far, these ideas are only theory; no one has yet set up such an organization or even explained precisely how it would work in actual practice. But the theory should not be dismissed without further consideration; if nothing else, it is at least a serious attempt to transform complex, largely impersonal organizations into more democratic institutions—a goal dreamed of by many now trapped in the toils of the system.

Assignment: the moon

In 1961 President John F. Kennedy committed the U.S. to the goal of landing a man on the moon before the decade ended. The undertaking, Project Apollo, was an assault of unparalleled magnitude on the unknown. No one knew if man could stand the strain of lunar flight, or even if the moon *could* be landed on: many scientists believed its surface to be soft dust that would swallow landing craft. If all the mysteries were to be solved and the goal achieved, the job of putting together the endeavor would be one of history's greatest organizational challenges.

That challenge was met in an unusual way: by setting up an organization of organizations. Rather than one big, centrally controlled operation, Apollo was many independent organizations guided by the tiny Washington, D.C., headquarters in the Office of Manned Space Flight of the National Aeronautics and Space Administration. There were never more than 30,000 NASA employees on the project, but it involved 400,000 other workers, granted 200 colleges $100 million for research, and awarded contracts to 16 major industrial firms and 20,000 subcontractors who built rockets and controls, trained astronauts, ran multiple tests and finally put men on the moon. This scheme achieved its seemingly impossible goal partly because of the organizational plan and partly because of other factors —glamor, ample funds, public support. But even this was not enough until a 1967 fire in an Apollo spaceship killed three astronauts. The accident, caused by defective design and careless workmanship, drew NASA and its contractors together with an almost mystic determination to conquer space.

Closing in on outer space, officials from NASA and its contractors face five supervisors at Cape Kennedy (which later resumed its earlier name, Cape Canaveral) at a meeting to coordinate efforts of the many elements making up Project Apollo. At these sessions anyone could report a hitch that might delay launch preparation.

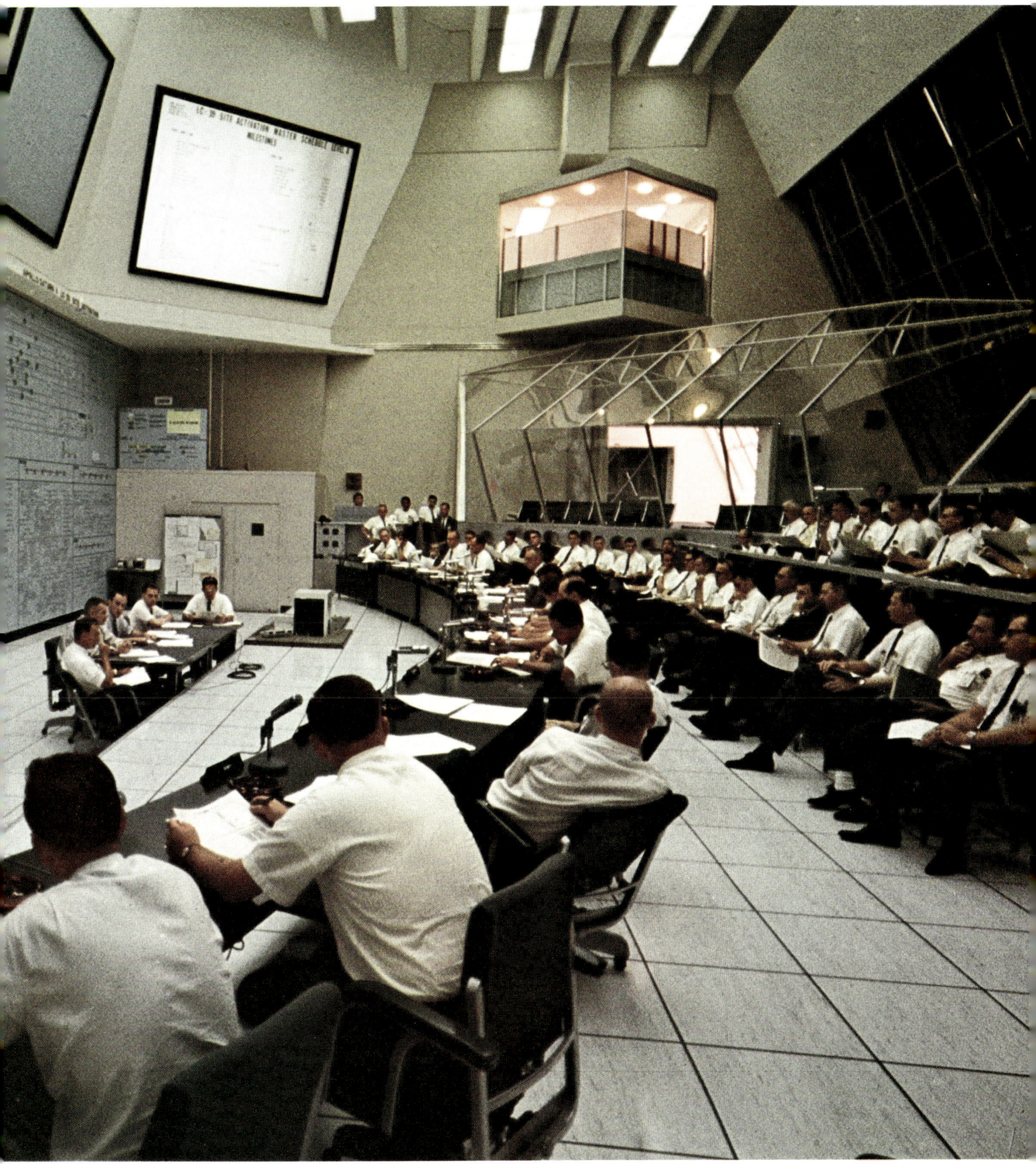
LC-39 SITE ACTIVATION MASTER SCHEDULE
MILESTONES

To build this 80-foot Saturn rocket section, Chrysler sent its workers to a government-owned assembly plant at Michoud, Louisiana

A system whose sole purpose is to test another system—a unit to check controls of a space module—is wired by a technician at Honeywell in Minneapolis. Each of these control devices was subjected to 7,700 hours of testing before it was shipped from the factory.

To forestall disaster, test upon test

On a trip that would last eight days and go 245,000 miles from a repair shop, failure of any crucial part was unthinkable. Most systems had backups with backups of their own. But much of the Apollo effort went into testing to make sure that even the first backup would prove to be unneeded.

These intricate tryout programs were supervised by a network of eight NASA offices at field centers and major contractors' plants. NASA also made sure all the parts came together right, coordinating production so that any change in a section produced at one plant—the weight, for instance—was compensated for in a section made elsewhere.

Still buoyant after 100-odd plunges from a 143-foot tower into a pool at North American Aviation's plant at Downey, California, a replica of a module bobs up after its simulated splashdown.

91

Because no one knew the spread of temperatures the lunar mission would encounter—estimated extremes went as low as −320° F. and as high as 350° F.— the durability of parts for space vehicles was tested over the whole range inside this giant simulator at a Douglas Aircraft plant in California

Experts from both sides of the Apollo team come together at Cape Kennedy, as specialists from New York's Grumman Corporation and from NASA supervise the intricate final assembly of a four-legged lunar landing module.

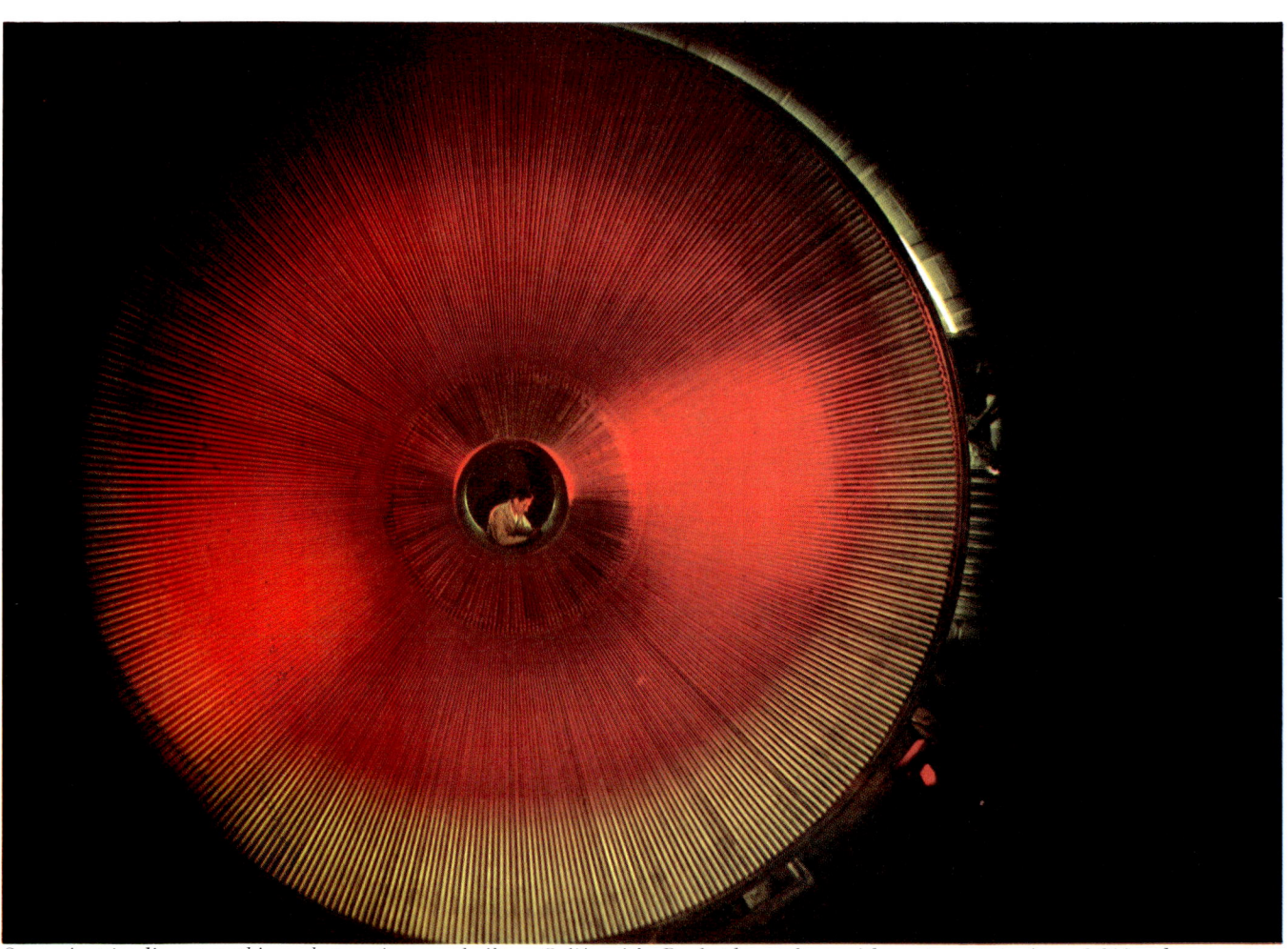

Seven feet in diameter, this rocket engine was built at California's Rocketdyne plant with parts sent in from 2,800 subcontractors.

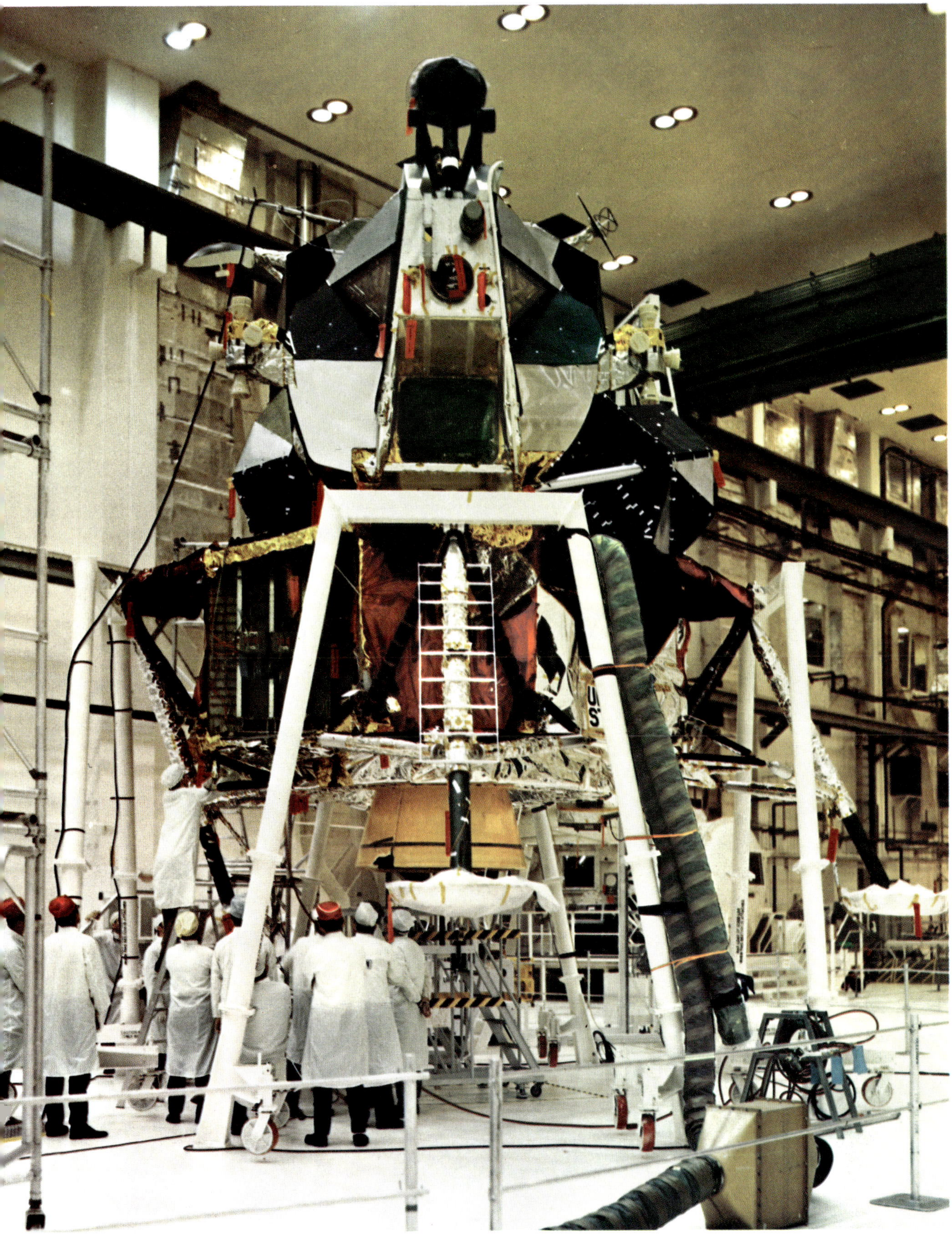

Learning to cope with zero gravity, three astronauts, watched by their teacher, float—momentarily weightless—as their plane drops.

Training to work in an alien world

Walking in a space suit over rough lava beds, floating freely during aerial acrobatics, spinning in a centrifuge's high acceleration—all were part of the training of Apollo astronauts. This attempt to prepare men for an environment that could not be exactly duplicated by any scheme on earth was one of the few Apollo programs completely operated, rather than supervised, by NASA itself.

But training, too, depended heavily on a constant interchange of ideas among the many organizations making up the big Apollo organization. Equipment designers, physiological researchers, lunar experts and, not least, the astronauts themselves all had to learn from one another.

Walter Cunningham, wearing an early space suit, steps gingerly over a lava bed in eastern Oregon. The ground was chosen for an astronaut training ground because it resembled lunar terrain.

94

Aboard a full-scale mockup of the lunar command module, Ed Aldrin (left) adjusts the controls for a practice landing while Neil Armstrong monitors the craft's position. Simulated flights like this one not only let the astronauts learn procedures but helped accustom them to the module's cramped quarters.

96

At Houston, two flight directors watch a third (foreground) guide an Apollo 9 flight.

Group advice, one-man decisions

Decisions on which the astronauts' lives depended had to be made in a matter of seconds—at Cape Kennedy during the launch and separately, over half a continent away, at Mission Control in Houston during flight. One man in each headquarters bore this frightening responsibility, but so complex were the questions raised that each depended on a small army of machines and men *(left)* to aid him.

Each launch was monitored by some 450 industry and NASA men gathered at Cape Kennedy to advise the launch director. Once the ship was airborne, space-flight specialists at Mission Control watched consoles, ready to help the flight director, one of three who alternated in round-the-clock shifts.

During a launch, technicians manning these 200 consoles at Cape Kennedy reported their observations to a test conductor. The conductor could then, if need be, buck the problem all the way to the launch director for decision.

97

The climactic step for the giant Apollo organization was man's first step on the moon. Here, on July 20, 1969, astronaut Neil Armstrong plants his ripple-soled boot in lunar dust. It was the act of one man, but it was closely followed by the multitudinous task force back on earth that had made it possible.

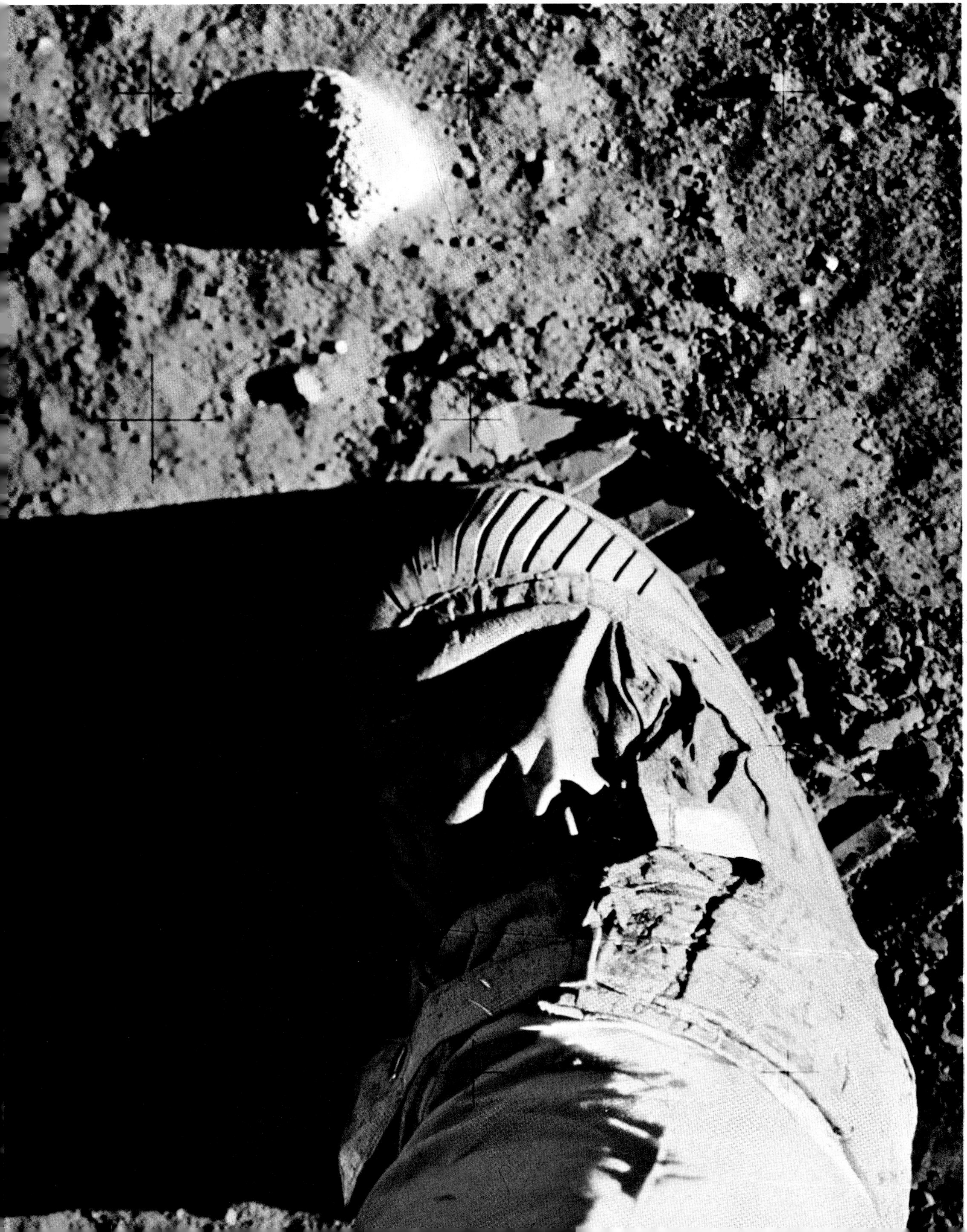

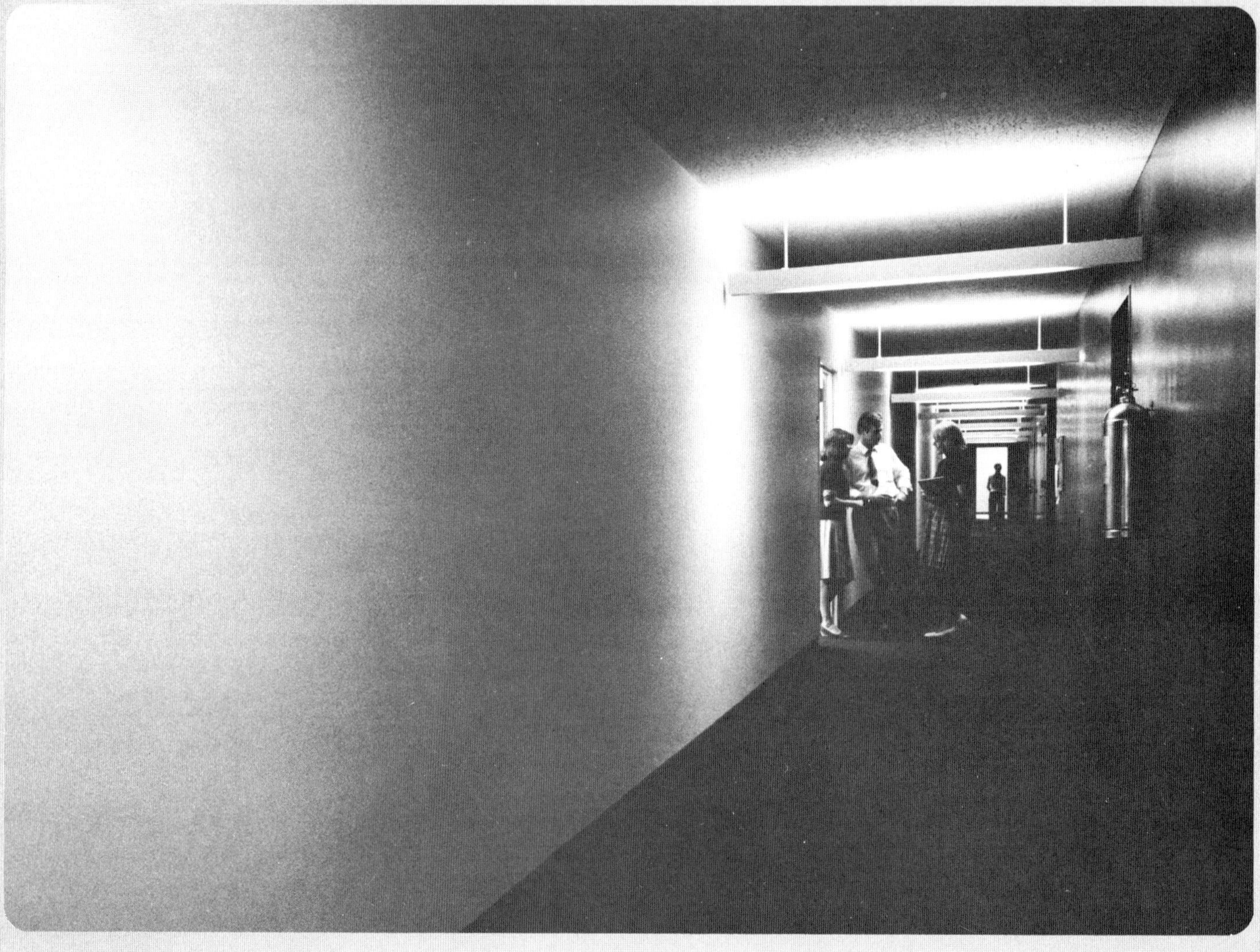

Behind the Scenes

Soon after he became President, John F. Kennedy sat in the Oval Office of the White House and listened to a visitor's suggestion. "That's a first-rate idea," said President Kennedy. Then, to the surprise of the visitor, he added, "Now we must see whether we can get the government to accept it."

As the head of that government Kennedy held more formal, visible power than any man on earth, and his visitor assumed that the President's command would make all the members of the federal bureaucracy scurry about instantly to carry out his wishes. But Kennedy himself knew that formal, Presidential authority, flowing down the bureaucratic pyramid from the White House, was not enough to put a plan into operation. Something more was necessary before a decision could be carried out. In the government, and in every large organization, another, invisible kind of power exists, as important as the official power. It is the power of the informal structure within the pyramid that can be called the organization's Inner Face. The Inner Face was what Kennedy was talking about when he said that he had to get "the government" to accept the idea.

The Inner Face of an organization, in the words of University of Massachusetts sociologist Charles Page, "consists of rules, groupings and sanctioned systems of procedure . . . they are never recorded in the codes or official blueprints . . . they are clearly and semipermanently established, they are just as 'real' and just as compelling on the membership as the elements of the official structure, and they maintain their existence and social significance throughout many changes of personnel."

The Inner Face includes several interrelated parts. Among them, and most important, is the informal group that inevitably takes shape whenever a number of people work together over a period of time. It is a network of personal and social relations that are not required by formal authority but arise spontaneously as people associate with one another. This informal group is not just a random collection of individuals inhabiting the same office or factory—although, because the group develops out of face-to-face contact between its members, it is usually confined to one level of the formal hierarchy, or two at the most. It commands loyalty, dispenses social satisfactions and enforces standards of behavior on its adherents. Each group has its own leaders and status systems, a role structure that is apart from the official one but obviously is influenced by it. As individuals come and go, the relationships between official roles and informal roles may change. The character of a particular group, and the amount of power it informally wields, fluctuates with time, although the group itself may continue to exist indefinitely.

A second feature of the Inner Face consists of unofficial rules that emerge within the organization from a general-sense of what is right and proper. Some of these rules may apply only within one informal group and may be primarily social—such as the tacit requirement that everyone in the crowd contribute something to a going-away present for a member, or the determination of who takes a turn at fetching coffee on Thursday. Other rules extend throughout many divisions and echelons of an organization and may regulate the way the job is done—the agreements on what constitutes a fair day's work, for instance, or when jobs may be traded, or which formal orders can be ignored. Unofficial rules often tend to be more permanent than official rules because they cannot be amended by fiat, but only by consensus.

The Inner Face also embodies unspoken but sanctified systems of procedure that the groups consider important to the smooth functioning of the organization. Most of these procedures merely amplify formal directives, guiding the members through situations that the formal rules do not cover, such as the accepted method for completing forms or submitting expense accounts. Other Inner Face procedures are designed to get around a rigid bureaucratic structure, enabling the organization to operate more sensibly and efficiently and with less strain on the individuals involved (i.e., an understanding about which forms can be dispensed with and what expense items deducted). Learning the ropes in an organization requires a newcomer to become acquainted with these semipermanent traditions, and he must depend on an informal group to teach him.

Taken together, these aspects of the Inner Face make up a shadow organization that may exert more authority than the formal one. Its inherent power was dramatically realized in Japan immediately after World War II. The Allied Occupation authorities had broken up the *zaibatsu*—the four huge business combines that had dominated the Japanese economy for decades—and purged some of their leaders from public life. Thenceforth, the Occupation decreed, the many divisions of each combine were to be independent companies. But the leaders of each *zaibatsu* group continued to meet, informally, and to make collective decisions that had no force in law but were rigorously followed because they were rooted in old allegiances. After the Occupation the *zaibatsu* reemerged, in altered form but with their economic influence almost undiminished.

The *zaibatsu*'s informal relations are still vital: The Mitsubishi Group, now the largest of the combines, is governed at the highest level by the heads of its 30 or so largest manufacturing, shipping, banking, real estate, insurance and export-import firms, who meet once each month. This gathering represents no formal structure, no overwhelming pattern of stock ownership. Legally it is nothing more than an informal group, a top-level manifestation of the Inner Face. But this group decides on major new investments by member firms, approves large foreign deals, chooses the companies to help out brother firms in trouble and generally determines policy for the entire combine. At Mitsubishi the formal structure is clearly under the control of the Inner Face.

The Inner Face operates at such exalted levels only when an exceptional circumstance like a military occupation makes leaders temporarily subordinate to some other authority. There is generally no need for sidestepping official procedures at the top—whatever procedures are used there can be the official ones. At lower levels in a complex and necessarily impersonal organization, the situation is quite different. There, Inner Face provides the means by which formal rules, roles and structure are translated into human terms so that human beings can operate them. A certain amount of tension inevitably exists between the Inner Face and the formal structure. This tension does not necessarily lead to conflict. Although the Inner Face may sometimes block the accomplishment of organization goals, it can often prevent an organization from becoming mired in its own regulations and complexity.

The human need for the Inner Face becomes evident to the recruit on his first day in the army, or to the brand-new employee of a large corporation or government bureaucracy. He arrives unknown. His face is not recognized. His interests and idiosyncracies are ignored by people he meets. Suddenly he is a number, an anonymous replaceable cog. Quite naturally, without thinking about it, he resists this depersonalization and strives to introduce a measure of humanity to his strange new world. The recruit may mutter a wisecrack about the sergeant to the next man in line; the new employee may introduce himself to someone at the next desk or ask a respectful question. Both newcomers seek friends, a social system to fit into, and they will observe others for clues on how to behave. When they have found these clues, and start to pattern their own behavior after the behavior of those around them, they have taken the first step toward joining the Inner Face.

Management professor Keith Davis of Arizona State University has described this almost universal need for companionship in *Human Behavior at Work*: "In a large office an employee may feel like only a payroll number, but his informal group gives him personal attachment and status. With them he is somebody, even though in the formal structure he is only one of 1,000 clerks. He may not look forward to posting 750 accounts daily, but the informal group can give more meaning to his day. When he can think of meeting his friends, sharing their jokes and eating with them, his day takes on a new dimension that makes easier any disagreeableness or routine in his work."

In these groups, University of California sociologist Robert Dubin comments, "The social character of man's personality is continually emphasized and re-enforced. It is here that each individual finds himself at the end of a work day still a man, a personality, and not reduced to the status of an adjunct to a machine."

Organization members have always been aware of the Inner Face they were part of, but until the 1930s neither administrators nor organization experts recognized its importance or even realized its existence. Many corporation managers simply gave orders and expected them to be obeyed without question; workers were often assumed to be interested only in getting more money for less work, and hence in need of close supervision. What changed these attitudes and revealed the Inner Face was a massive study of the employees and work practices at a Western Electric Company plant in Hawthorne, Illinois.

The Hawthorne investigation, now regarded as a landmark in the study of organizational behavior, began in the mid-1920s. After a time the company called upon a research group including a Harvard Business School professor, Elton Mayo, to solve a mystery. Western Electric had conducted tests to find out what effect changes in lighting would have on the speed of assembly and inspection of small electrical parts. The executives were puzzled by the results they got. As they had expected, production rose

In a test that revised concepts of forces within an organization, women at Western Electric's Hawthorne Works in Chicago assemble telephone relays (left). As each assembly lands in a chute, completion time is recorded. A team led by Harvard's Elton Mayo (above) monitored this output from 1927 to 1932 under good and bad working conditions. Regardless of conditions, productivity kept rising. The women, stimulated by their special status, had become a prolific task force.

when illumination was increased, but then—to their surprise—it continued to rise when the lighting was dimmed. Furthermore, a control group of workers, whose illumination was not changed at all, had increased their production almost as much as those whose lights were varied.

To discover what was happening, Harvard and Western Electric researchers began a detailed study of six experienced women workers specially selected and assigned to a separate room to assemble components, called relays, for telephone equipment. The group's output was measured against every conceivable factor that could influence productivity: lighting, room temperature, the length and number of rest periods and holidays, pay rates and the arrangement of the work itself. Every time the researchers altered these conditions they interviewed each worker thoroughly, carefully noting her reactions to the changes. Soon it became apparent that, except for minor fluctuations that occurred after each innovation, the overall productivity of the group was rising markedly and steadily, and so was morale.

"In many respects these results were puzzling to the investigators," said one report on the experiment, "for they were not what they had expected. The general upward trend in output independent of any particular change in rest pauses or shorter working hours was astonishing. The improvement of mental attitude throughout the first two years was also perplexing." It took two more years of fruitless experiments before the researchers realized that the explanation lay in the Inner Face.

In the first place, the women were fairly homogeneous in age, social status, education and work experience. Two of them, good friends, had chosen the others when the experiment began. Furthermore, by the very act of setting up the Relay Assembly Test Room, the investigators had bypassed many of the normal bureaucratic rules of the factory and given the women a different status from that of the other workers. As a result, "a new type of spontaneous social organization developed. Social conditions had been established which allowed the operators to develop their own values and objectives. The experimental conditions allowed the operators to develop openly social codes at work and these codes, unhampered by interference, gave a sustained meaning to their work." The operators formed "a group, or informal organization, which could be characterized as a network of personal relations which had been developed in and through a particular way of working together; it was an organization that not only satisfied the wishes of its members but also worked in harmony with the aims of management." Thus the researchers—although they did not use the term—discovered the existence of the Inner Face and its strength; they concluded that "the limits of human collaboration are determined far more by the informal than by the formal organization of the plant."

Once the Hawthorne researchers recognized the importance of the Inner Face, they went on to learn more about it. This time, instead of manipulating working conditions, they merely observed and recorded the social interactions and work patterns of a group of 14 men wiring and soldering terminals on telephone switchboard banks. In this experiment, known as the Bank Wiring Observation Room, the researchers found that the men quickly arranged themselves into two cliques—each made up of men who worked closely together—and several workers who did not belong permanently to either one. The clique composed of "the group in front" enjoyed more prestige and its members looked down on "the group in back" because the front clique worked faster. Because each clique included two classes of workers—some who wired the apparatus, along with others, lower paid and less skilled, who merely soldered—it was apparent to the researchers that proximity was more important to the formation of informal groups than job status or rank.

The relative prestige of the two cliques showed up in a number of subtle ways. The men in front disparaged the back clique. The men in back were constantly arguing among themselves about whether a window should be open or closed; the front clique disdained such controversies. During rest periods or interruptions in the flow of work, the men in back indulged in horseplay while those in front tended to make bets, match coins and play cards. And though they all bought snacks from the same canteen, those of the front clique purchased a more expensive kind of chocolate—but in small quantity compared to the amount of the cheaper kind favored by workers in the back clique.

The most significant aspect of this Inner Face behavior concerned productivity. The men were not paid by the hour but by the piece—so much for each bank completed. Both groups quickly established a norm, a level of output to be maintained as a fair day's work—and it was the same in each group, two switchboard banks per man per day. They kept the average rate of production at or just below that level despite the piecework system, which would have netted them more money if they had worked faster. The men felt that if they produced too much, management would either reduce the piece-rate bonus or lay off some of the workers. On the other hand, if they produced less, the decline in production would cost an unacceptable reduction in their take-home pay.

Generally, the men of the seemingly superior front clique kept very close to company requirements and rarely falsified their production records; their higher status compelled them to conform to formal rules. The men of the back clique produced less, claimed more and put in for more off-time allowances [blamed on faulty equipment or materials]; according to one analysis that was their way of protesting their inferior reputations. The most popular man in the room—a natural leader and a member of the front clique—and another worker who was trying to become a leader of the back clique maintained daily production rates that were closest to the norm, while two unpopular men who belonged to neither clique managed to violate the norm by turning out a little more than two banks a day. But the unceasing discipline of the Inner Face prevented these individual variations from straying too far from the recognized standard. Rate-busters, the men who worked too fast, and chiselers, those who did not work hard enough, were subtly or openly punished—by ridicule, sarcastic remarks that everyone could hear, occasional ostracism or, usually in the back-of-the-room, low-status clique, an occasional punch to the upper arm. The penalties, as well as the rewards, seemed to work.

In much of the literature on organizational behavior, this case study and later ones like it are cited as evidence that the Inner Face restricts production. That is only half of the truth. The unofficial rules of the Bank Wiring Observation Room also assured that production was kept up to a level that was profitable for both workers and management; the managers of the Hawthorne plant were entirely satisfied with the output of the group. The real lesson of the Hawthorne study was that the Inner Face is a power structure with its own goals, which neither management nor individual workers can overrule.

The power of the Inner Face derives primarily from its ability to reward with acceptance those who follow its rules and to discipline members who go astray. Just as the official structure can cut an erring member off from the organization's benefits, by firing an employee or excommunicating a believer, the ultimate punishment of the Inner Face is ostracism, thus isolating an offender from the social benefits of the group. In Britain a worker who violates the group's standards may find that none of his erstwhile friends will talk to him, eat with him or acknowledge his presence—sometimes for months on end. In one celebrated case, a British locomotive engineer committed suicide after living in such silence for a year. When Englishmen ostracize an individual they say they are "sending him to Coventry," an expression dating to the 17th Century. At that time the citizens of the town of Coventry hated the King's soldiers and refused to speak to anyone in uniform; military commanders who wanted to discipline a man would send him to the Coventry garrison, where he had to live in social isolation.

Such social cruelty is hardly a British monopoly, but in the more mobile society of the United States a worker who is subjected to that sort of sanction can—at least in times of prosperity—move to another town or look for another job. At the U.S. Military Academy at West Point, however, many generations of cadets punished suspected violators of their honor code with a now-abandoned form of ostracism that was known as The Silence *(page 109)*.

A banished member, however, is no longer under Inner Face control, so such extreme punishment is only levied as a last resort, or when the violation is particularly heinous. Frequent ostracism would decimate the group and encourage the formation of a rival clique made up of outcasts. Therefore the more usual punishments are milder, including many of the natural things that people do when they are angry at somebody: giving curt answers to questions, making sarcastic remarks, finding fault, purposely neglecting a customary friendly ritual. These little social slaps may be tolerable when they come from just one angry friend, but they sting much more sharply and are much more effective when they are administered by several people ganging up on a miscreant and laughing or sneering together at his shame.

Sociologist Peter Blau of Columbia University, who studied workings of the federal bureaucracy in Washington, reported that when a group of colleagues laugh together at aggressive remarks directed against an individual, the victim is "momentarily put into the worst state of anomie: being alone and feeling disoriented while witnessing the cohesiveness of others. This threat constituted a strong inducement to surrender unorthodox opinions and to cease deviant practices."

Since all these sanctions involve some degree of exclusion, it follows that they work only when the sense of belonging to the informal group matters to the individual—that is, when he feels loyal to it. This same loyalty also can compel an individual to sacrifice himself for the group even without the threat of sanctions.

Such a loyal sacrifice is made by the combat soldier who blindly, almost wildly, charges an enemy position in the face of certain death and in defiance of prudent orders. Propagandists may attribute this kind of heroism to patriotism or to hatred of the enemy, but every man who has seen combat, and every surviving hero, knows that these extraordinary acts are really motivated by elemental loyalty to the men in the unit, by the individual's desire to help or save his buddies.

Loyalty to a group of peers—as distinguished from loyalty to an idea or to a leader—is the glue that holds the Inner Face together. It springs from two sources, social compatibility and shared experience; wherever the Inner Face is powerful, both are present. Social compatibility depends on similar factors in the individuals' backgrounds that enable those people to cooperate and get along easily with one another; education, religion, social status, age, and political and moral beliefs. Unfortunately for the ideal of equality, race and sex also belong on this list. An organization may formally abolish color or sex discrimination, but individuals may still encounter prejudice and chauvinism because the tight face-to-face groups of the Inner Face deny full membership to people who are different. One extreme example is the persistent refusal of many American construction unions to admit blacks to their ranks. Policemen's organizations that resist the assignment of policewomen to patrol duties are following the same pattern.

Most of the time the tests of social compatibility are more subtle and are applied to individuals rather than to entire classes of the population. One management expert believes that "Men often will not work at all, and will rarely work well, under other incentives if the social situation from their point of view is unsatisfactory. Thus often men of inferior education cannot work well with those of superior education, and vice versa.... A powerful incentive to the effort of almost all men is favorable associational conditions."

The need for compatibility becomes more apparent at the executive lev-

His diploma in hand, West Pointer James Pelosi smiles with quiet pride after enduring 19 months of ostracism by his classmates.

The survival of an outcast

When James J. Pelosi entered the United States Military Academy at West Point in 1969, he quickly became popular with his classmates and was nominated to the prestigious Cadet Honor Committee. In his third year, this auspicious start turned sour as Pelosi angered the informal "inside" structure that, in the Academy as in all organizations, holds major power. Accused of disobeying examination rules, Pelosi was summoned before the honor committee. He denied the accusations; but the committee found him guilty. Although West Point's superintendent dismissed the case and reinstated him to good standing, the committee refused to exonerate him. Lacking Academy authority, his peers resorted to the punishment commonly used on those who defy the informal Inner Face: ostracism, then known at West Point as The Silence. Such treatment has since been abandoned at the Point, but in the past it forced cadets to resign; Pelosi stuck it out.

For the next 19 months, Pelosi's fellow cadets rarely spoke to him except on official business. He roomed and ate alone. His mail was torn up, and his possessions were vandalized. Only upon his graduation in June 1973, did his ordeal end. "It was just as if I were a person again," he said. How did he survive ostracism? He read, worked out in the gym, struck up conversations with MPs and kept a journal. Still, Pelosi lost 26 pounds during The Silence, and at times he feared the ordeal would affect his military career.

el, where intangibles of personality sometimes seem to be more important than formal qualifications. At the upper echelons of any organization pyramid, formal authority and Inner Face authority converge, as the individuals responsible for granting promotions also act as a screening committee for their informal executive group. Therefore, often unwittingly, they may pay a good deal more attention to the assortment of factors that will determine how well a candidate fits into the Inner Face—manners, politics, religion, leisure activities, college affiliation—than to how well he or she can perform on the job.

Even if all the members fit into it socially, the Inner Face will not win their loyalty until they share experiences, triumphs, even dangers. When Columbia University professor Charles Frankel became Assistant Secretary of State for Educational and Cultural Affairs in the Lyndon Johnson administration, he discovered that the group loyalty within the Foreign Service frequently prevented him from hiring people he wanted: the Inner Face usually found someone else it considered more deserving. In his book *High on Foggy Bottom*, Frankel analyzed this loyalty:

"People who have done difficult things together, who have seen one another tested . . . are bound to one another by memory and sentiment. People who have gone through a crisis in Brazil or Yemen in each other's company, or who have stood side by side under the pummeling of a Congressional Appropriations Committee, come out with feelings toward each other that transcend personal advantage or disadvantage, ideological agreement or disagreement. . . . The loyalties of members of the Foreign Service go out to one another. They have a common and unusual relation to the world and a common set of problems. They have to worry about the education of their children in foreign countries; about servants abroad and high prices in Washington; about the separation of families, the temperament of the ambassador's wife and orders that send them where they don't want to go. . . . They have been called cookie pushers *and* Communists, the architects of American globalism *and* the agents of foreign countries—and sometimes by one and the same man . . . they have a sense of being misunderstood and persecuted, which enhances the Service's inner cohesion."

Inner Face loyalty and solidarity is naturally more noticeable when it comes into contention with the formal leadership than when it quietly does the job. This subtle kind of conflict surfaced when Frankel outlined to a subordinate a new method of dealing with a particular problem and directed the man to put it into effect. The underling did nothing and later explained his inaction by telling Frankel, "It occurred to me after I left your office that you hadn't thought through all the implications of what you were saying"—namely, that "we've been doing it the other way for twenty years." When Frankel insisted, he discovered that he was attacking more than just a policy. "I was attacking a creed, an organization's faith." In defending his stand, the subordinate "didn't say 'I,' he said 'We.' He meant all the people with whom he had worked through all the years, all the people who had developed the old policy and believed in it. Was I indifferent to everything that they had done and suffered? Was I saying that, for all that time, they had been wrong? Was I asking him to be disloyal to them? . . . He wasn't so much refusing to do what I wanted as saying he couldn't do it. His reflexes didn't work that way." Frankel also discovered that the insiders had a phrase to describe the phenomenon: officials who tried to push a new policy against the views of the Inner Face were accused of "getting too far out in front of the Department."

Resistance against directives that threaten informal procedure is more prevalent in government bureaucracies than in corporations for the simple reason that civil servants cannot be easily fired. But it would be a mistake to assume that the Inner Face of government always is antagonistic to the organization's formal system of operation. For much if not most of the time the bureaucratic Inner Face actually helps the organization achieve its principal purposes.

Among the many ways the Inner Face expresses itself is the technique of beating the system, that is, deliberately circumventing—even violating—official rules of procedure. Almost everyone in a large organization uses such stratagems, and they are sometimes so petty that their significance is not realized. The purchasing department of one large New York corporation, for instance, refuses to buy the kind of transparent tape that can be written upon, claiming it is too expensive. But the tape can save time for the editors and writers—and therefore for the company—so employees simply buy it and charge the company for it by submerging the cost in their expense accounts. Another concern gave a group of employees time off to watch the local baseball team when it played a home game; the workers agreed among themselves to come in an hour early on those days to make up the lost time. Individual workers who were not that well motivated, and who objected to the early start, found themselves under Inner Face pressure to conform, and conform they did.

Just how important and beneficial these minor irregularities can become, when added up, is evident when railroad or post-office employees discontinue their normal practice of beating the system to "work by the book" during a labor dispute. Then, with everyone carefully obeying every formal regulation to the letter, trains run hours late, mail piles up and the tempers of the citizens boil over. Efficiency is restored when the Inner Face procedures go into effect once more.

Sometimes, beating the system merely consists of getting around an individual bottleneck. Here the method used must be suited to that individual's personality. During the Korean War, correspondents found a way to move their stories quickly through a censoring officer who always cut something out of every story, even the most innocuous one. When that officer was on duty, the correspondents passed the word to one another, and anybody filing a story would insert some blatant violation of military security. The censor would cut out the deliberately offending passage and

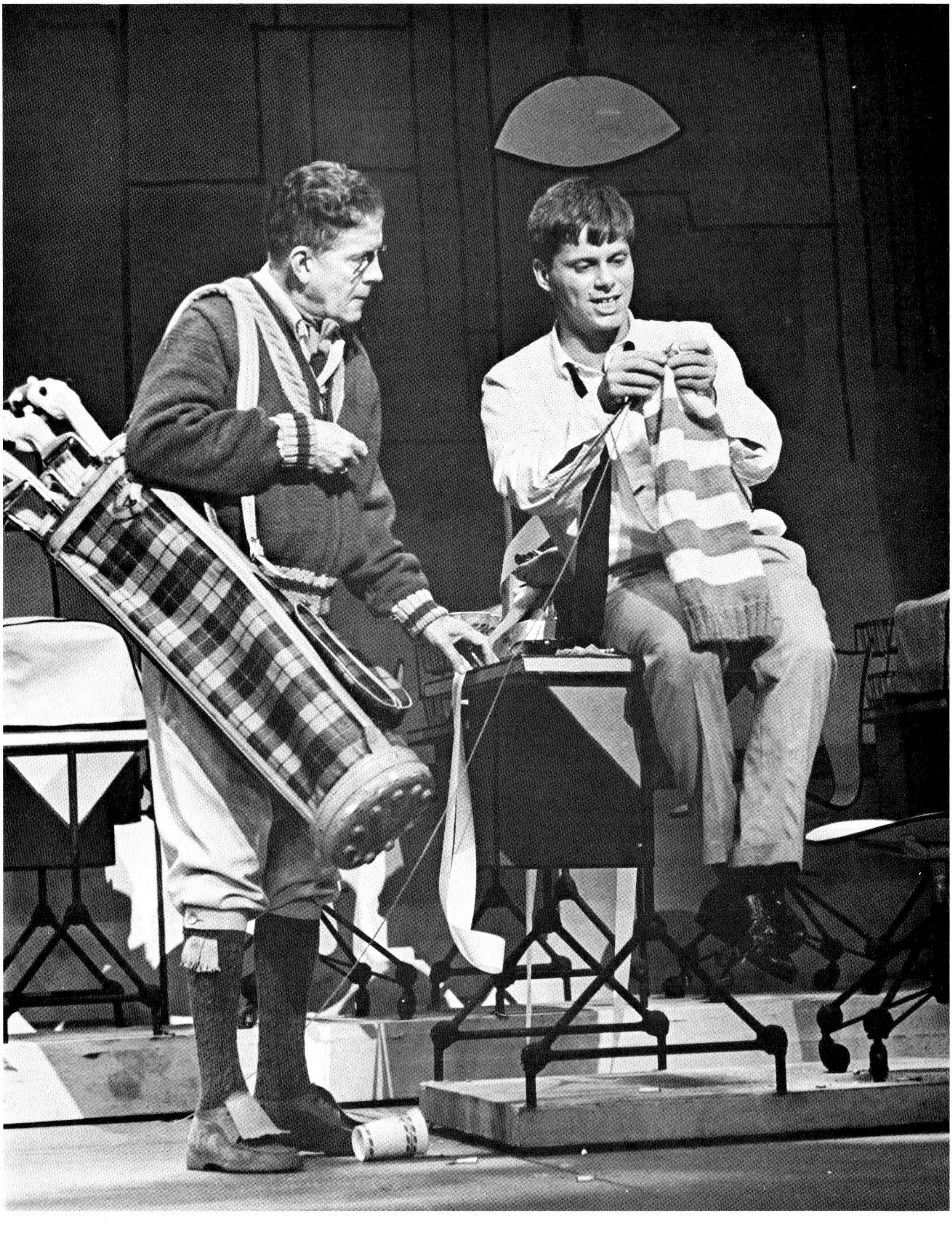

In a lesson from the musical spoof, "How to Succeed in Business without Really Trying," on-the-make employee Finch (Robert Morse) shows how to climb the ladder fast by playing to the hobby of boss Biggley (Rudy Vallee):
B: What's that you're doing?
F: I guess it looks silly, sir. But . . . knitting helps me think more clearly.
B: Well, I'll be damned. I knit, too. . . .
F: I feel kind of sorry for men who don't knit. They lead empty lives.
B: I like the way you think, Finch . . . what's your ambition in this outfit? . . .

then let the rest of the story pass without much more than a passing glance.

In the State Department, Charles Frankel became a sort of bottleneck in the eyes of his subordinates, and their Inner Face found a way to bypass him. Objecting to the vague, buck-passing gobbledygook in the letters that were brought to his desk for signature, Frankel set out to improve their prose and tone. Quickly, Frankel relates, his staff collected a file of " 'cleared paragraphs' . . . collected from letters that I had written myself, or that had got by me without my raising an objection. By the judicious shuffling of cleared paragraphs, a letter could be prepared for my signature that I could not, it was believed, send back." This scheme was one that did not work too well: "Letters constructed out of cleared paragraphs, forthright and unequivocal though they might be, often didn't answer the questions asked."

Beating the system for personal gain often becomes embedded in the sanctified procedures of the Inner Face. In *Working*, a book of interviews about jobs in America, Studs Terkel quotes a gas-meter reader who regularly completes his daily rounds in about four hours instead of the eight hours he is paid to work. The informal rules let him get away with this: "My boss and the boss before him were meter readers and they would have the same book as I had. What was usually an eight-hour day took them four hours, so they're not gonna rat on me." (He also revealed some of the Inner Face codes the meter readers write in their list of customers: code nine, for people who object if you walk on their lawns; Q for "cutie," a good-looking young woman —"Then the guy'll stop and read the house for sure.")

Such petty subterfuges humanize the organization, giving its authoritarian structure and codified procedures the flexibility to compensate for individual frailty, operate by common sense and adapt quickly to circumstances. There are times, however, when the rules must be bent in a much more serious way. Such attempts to act unofficially may carry grave risks, for if the action does not achieve an acceptable result, the failure may so upset the official system that severe punishment is almost certain (for violation of regulations, not failure of the action). Willingness to accept such risks, when the situation demands, tests the power of the Inner Face and, ultimately, the courage and convictions of its supporters.

Peter Blau observed the way the Inner Face in one federal bureau neatly balanced its procedures against the system's so that a potentially dangerous confrontation was avoided and both sides benefited. The agency involved was charged with enforcing a particular piece of New Deal legislation. Whenever a businessman tried to bribe one of the agency's inspectors, the inspector was, according to official regulations, required to report the attempt to his superiors. Failure to do so would itself be a crime. But the agents' own informal code strictly prohibited such reports because the men considered reporting bribes to be a bid for promotion or other official recognition. Their code insisted that an agent squelch bribery overtures long before they reached the stage of an outright offer, and

DEPARTMENT OF THE ARMY
HEADQUARTERS, PICATINNY ARSENAL
DOVER, NEW JERSEY 07801

SARPA-CP   25 Jan 74

Dear Mr. Berger:

Your Suggestion No. H34-74   Subject: Removal of silver tip on
Retractable Ball-Point Pens
which was referred to primary interested agencies for evaluation, was not
recommended for adoption. Reasons for this decision by the evaluator(s)
are given in the attached comments.

Although your suggestion was not given favorable consideration, the
interest and initiative you displayed in submitting it are appreciated.

Ideas received through the Army Suggestion Plan have resulted in benefits
of many millions of dollars to the government, improvement in morale and
elimination of numerous safety hazards.

You are urged to continue your participation in the Army Suggestion Plan.
Let your ideas be for Economy - Safety - Progress.

SUGGESTION EVALUATION
For use of this form, see CPPM 1, Sec 12; the proponent agency is Office of the Deputy Chief of Staff for Personnel.

TO: (Include ZIP Code)	FROM: (Include ZIP Code)
Incentive Awards Administrator SMUPA-CP, Bldg 118	Acting Chief, Station Supply & Stock Control Division, Bldg 91

1. SUGGESTION TITLE: Removal of Silver Tip on Retractable Ball-Point Pens
2. SUGGESTION NUMBER: H-34-74

3. ACTION TAKEN OR RECOMMENDED
- a. APPROVED FOR ADOPTION □ TOTALLY □ PARTIALLY OR WITH MODIFICATION
- DATE SUGGESTION WAS OR WILL BE PUT INTO EFFECT □ ALSO RECOMMEND CONSIDERATION FOR WIDER APPLICATION AS INDICATED IN ITEM 4.
- b. ALREADY IN USE OR UNDER CONSIDERATION.
- c. RECOMMEND ADOPTION, BUT APPROVAL NOT WITHIN JURISDICTION OF THIS OFFICE.
- XX d. NOT RECOMMENDED FOR ADOPTION FOR REASONS SHOWN IN ITEM 4.
- e. OTHER (Specify in Item 4)

4. REASONS FOR ACTION TAKEN OR RECOMMENDED:
This suggestion is not recommended for adoption in accordance with
inclosed evaluation by General Services Administration.

UNITED STATES OF AMERICA
GENERAL SERVICES ADMINISTRATION

DATE: 12-12-73
REPLY TO ATTN OF: BPOR

Office of Administration
Washington, D.C. 20405

SUBJECT: Suggestion No. H-34-74

Mrs. Marie Lee (IDR)
Adjutant General Center
Department of the Army
ATTN: DAAG-ASO-P
Room GA159, Forrestal Bldg.
Washington, DC 20314

We are returning an employee suggestion which was forwarded to General Services Administration
for evaluation.

The suggestion has been evaluated and has not been recommended for adoption. The reasons are
given in the enclosed evaluation.

Although the suggestion was not recommended for adoption, we appreciate the time and thought
the suggestor has given this suggestion.

FRANCIS E. CAMMARATA
Central Office Suggestion Coordinator

Enclosures
Our File No. OA 74-127

Suggestion No: OA 74-12
Date Referred: 10/31/73

EVALUATION

The suggester alleges that the metal plunger and metal band ar
needed and should be eliminated thereby saving material and m

The ball point pens are designed to be serviceable during the li
of several refills. The metal parts are intended to improve the
performance, serviceability and aesthetic value of the pens.

Prior to revision of GG-B-0060C, the Government received num
complaints about the quality of the pens. Revision "C" of subjec
specification was developed and issued after extensive consultati
with industry and Federal agencies. From the response, it appe
that the majority of the users are now satisfied with the design,
quality, aesthetic value, and cost of the pens.

This office is aware of the apparent savings that could be realize
redesigning and changing some of the requirements of the pens.
are in contact with industry and have initiated a testing project wi
the intent of finding ways of improving the quality of the pens and
reducing cost. After further study, we will implement those chan
that will decrease the cost of the pens, provided these changes wil
not impair the quality and aesthetic value of the pens. Future chan
cannot be attributed to this or previous suggestions.

Adoption of this suggestion is not

MEMORANDUM

DEPARTMENT OF HEALTH, EDUCATION, AND WELFARE
SOCIAL SECURITY ADMINISTRATION

DATE: January
REFER TO: IAD 24

TO: Mr. Louis Zawatzky

FROM: Frank G. Matejik

SUBJECT: Highlight Report for the Week Ending January 4, 1974

<u>ITEMS RECOMMENDED FOR THE COMMISSIONER</u>

None

<u>ITEMS FOR THE ASSISTANT COMMISSIONER</u>

IV. Continuing activities:
  1. Negative

Gary E. Good
for Frank G. Matejik

ILLINOIS DEPARTMENT OF LABOR
BUREAU OF EMPLOYMENT SECURITY

MEMORANDUM

Date: April 30, 1971

To: David Gassman
Statistician II   Office:

From: Benjamin Greenstein, Chief
Research and Statistics   Office:

Subject: Hazardous Use of Coffee Pot

The afternoon of April 29, while Mr. Arthur Haverly was on vacation, an electric coffee pot was plugged in in his office and left unattended. It spread noxious fumes through the office and scorched a table belonging to the State.

You admitted that you plugged in that coffee pot and that you did it, although Mr. Haverly had told you that I had requested that it should not be done due to previous adverse experience. When I asked you why you plugged in that coffee pot, although I had requested that it should not be done, you stated that you did not take it that seriously.

I may note also that Mr. Haverly informed me the previous day that he had not authorized you to connect the coffee pot in his office.

The following facts, therefore, emerge:

1. You had used your supervisor's office for cooking coffee without his authorization.

2. You did so, although you knew that I had requested that it should not be done.

3. You had left the coffee pot unattended. For that matter, there may have been a conflict between performing agency work and attending to the coffee pot.

4. You created a fire hazard for your fellow workers and subjected them to noxious fumes.

5. When I asked you why you plugged in the coffee pot in spite of my request to the contrary, you stated that you did not take it that seriously. This is a rejection of supervision.

6. Your disregard of my authority has resulted in discomfort to your fellow workers and damage to State property.

7. On April 30, the day following the above actions and conversation, at 8:25 in the morning, I noted that you had again plugged in the coffee pot. When I pointed out that you were aware that I had asked you not to plug it in, you replied that it is not 8:30 yet. I then told you that I am in charge of the section, even though it is not 8:30 yet.

What should be done with respect to your actions, as specified above, is under consideration. In the meantime you are emphatically requested not to repeat the hazard you created by plugging in the coffee pot.

Benjamin Greenstein
BENJAMIN GREENSTEIN, Chief
Research and Statistics

Classics from a memo collection

As any lowly, hard-pressed mail clerk knows, communication in any big organization is carried on largely via the interoffice memorandum. Many are just inane. Some seem contrived only to keep the authors busy writing memos. But the examples reproduced here, selected from *The Washington Monthly*, a newsmagazine that runs a "Memo of the Month" and that has assembled a whole book of them, prove the versatility of the medium.

Memos can be used to note productivity, or the lack of it *(above)*. They can relate the history of a personality conflict *(right)*. Yet sometimes their overcomplication can be more apparent than real. The series at left, involving many levels of the federal bureaucracy, records the necessary and logical handling of a matter that—because the organization is so big—could involve the expenditure of millions.

anyone who violated this norm was unofficially castigated and ostracized.

By firmly fending off yet not reporting bribery approaches, the inspectors were better able to do their primary job. As incorruptible but not vindictive officials they could persuade the businessmen to comply with the law; accusations of bribery would have antagonized the business community and made these voluntary concessions more difficult to obtain. Blau concluded: "The prosecution of employers who tried to bribe civil servants, which was not a basic objective of this agency, would have interfered with the accomplishment of its own objectives. The taboo on reporting bribes, although contrary to an official rule, not only facilitated the task of agents but also contributed to the achievement of the goals of this agency." Yet the personal risks to the individual agent were always present. If he did not perceive a bribery situation developing, and act quickly but discreetly to head it off, he might be caught between violating a law and incurring the anger of his colleagues.

The risks are much greater when open disregard of ordinarily essential rules seems necessary. In Sicily during World War II, General George S. Patton's Seventh Army was about to launch an attack on Palermo when it received an order to move in a different direction and secure its flank before taking the city. Patton felt that his forces could and should take Palermo quickly. His chief of staff, Brigadier General Hobart R. Gay, told higher headquarters that part of the order had been garbled in transmission and asked that it be sent again, certain that by the time the order arrived for the second time the assault on Palermo would already be underway. Such connivance to flout a legitimate order took self-confidence and guts, qualities for which both Patton and Gay were noted. Patton was certain the attack would succeed, but if it had not, he would have been disgraced and Gay might have been court-martialed. But their daring succeeded—or at least their luck held—and the American Army gained itself a headline victory in Sicily.

The official system is so seldom contravened by one individual or a few acting alone that it is not difficult to understand why those who succeed are looked upon as heroes. Usually the power of the Inner Face depends on members—it generally includes enough people in enough places to prevent actions it considers objectionable and assist actions it considers desirable. But the influence of a large group can be effective only if its members can communicate readily with one another. To supply this need for fast information, the Inner Face has a superbly efficient communications system: the grapevine.

Every organization has one grapevine (or several). Keith Davis, who has made a study of them, observes that "if employees are so uninterested in their work that they do not engage in shoptalk about it, they are probably maladjusted. If employees are so uninterested in their associates that they do not exchange talk about who will likely get the next promotion or who recently had a baby, they probably are abnormal."

The word grapevine was first used to describe rumor networks during the Civil War, when telegraph lines were strung on trees like vines. Since many messages came through garbled, rumors were said to come from the grapevine. Today the word refers not just to rumor but to any unofficial communication system.

The efficiency of the organization grapevine derives from the shared knowledge and assumptions of the Inner Face. The fact that "Harry spent a half hour with the old man this afternoon" is only significant to those who have some ideas why Harry may be in trouble. In a well-integrated organization, management consultant Antony Jay has written, the grapevine "ensures that information gets quickly to the person who needs it. It means that as soon as the office boy sees the factory inspector's car, he rings Bill to tell him to put the safety hood over the chain drive in No. 3 shop. . . . It means the incoming stores checking clerk warns the turning foreman that the two-inch, mild steel bar still hasn't arrived, instead of letting him find out for himself when he needs it next week. It means that people know everyone else's job and needs as well as their own, and are collectively using the communication network to facilitate the operation."

Prestige as well as news is carried on the grapevine. Grapevine communication flows because one person knows something that another doesn't, and gains prestige by telling about it. His knowledge is proof that he is alert and well informed, and the recipient must pay him something in return, if only deference. Furthermore, the new possessor of the secret can also cash in on it by telling others. Thus, as sociologist Wilbert Moore points out, the secret speeds on because "the value attached to its confidential character has assured both attention and repetition."

A grapevine operates in clusters. One person may tell three or four people the news, but only one or two of them—usually insecure individuals who crave that extra fillip of status—pass it on. Thus, for any given bit of information, only a few people are active communicators. In one documented case, 68 per cent of the executives in a company had heard a bit of information but only 20 per cent of them had spread it.

The grapevine can also link the Inner Face to the formal structure. Alert administrators listen to the grapevine to find out what is on their employees' minds and to float trial balloons or broadcast information with which they don't want to be officially associated. One useful device in this situation is the "two-way funnel," a person who can be counted on to spread quickly any information that comes his way. Chosen because he already enjoys a reputation for knowing inside information, the funnel is particularly helpful in carrying unofficial communiqués between two competing or conflicting factions. If the ploy fails, face always can be saved by blaming "that unreliable rumor-monger."

The ploy can work more often than not, because the grapevine is surprisingly accurate. In normal situations, says Keith Davis, more than three fourths of the information passed along the grapevine is true. "People tend to think the grapevine is less accurate than it really is," he says, "be-

Chapter 4

cause its errors are more dramatic and consequently more impressed on memory than its day-to-day accuracy. Moreover, the inaccurate parts are often more important." One grapevine, for example, spread the story that a welder was going to marry the general manager's daughter, complete with the time and place of the wedding. The story was 90 per cent true: The bride-to-be, however, was not the general manager's daughter, but someone else with the same last name.

In all the ways the Inner Face carries out its varied functions—transmitting news up and down the grapevine, humanizing the impersonal system, sweeping aside bureaucratic obstacles, uniting a work force—it serves as a conservative force. It preserves traditional ways of doing things and resists pressures for change from this faction or that, inside or outside the organization. It guards old rituals and may invent new ones, for rituals themselves buttress conservatism.

Inner Face rituals provide a platform of certainty at times when change is inevitable and reassure the worriers that the world is not about to end. Office Christmas parties, holidays, tasks perpetuated beyond their usefulness, procedures involving filling out of forms and gathering multiple signatures all have a ritual significance that often seems puzzling or meaningless to the outsider. British Army clerks who spend hours typing details from a form onto a soldier's record card—although they could staple the form to the card in seconds—carry out a ritual meaningless to all but themselves.

In Bernard Malamud's novel *A New Life*, college professors make a fetish of the speed and efficiency with which they get their grade reports in every term—a ritual to hide from themselves the emptiness and banality of their teaching. In the opinion of some observers, even formal corporate training and testing programs that lead to promotions may serve many as rites of passage, for they don't always impart new skills or knowledge. They, like all rituals, inculcate in the participants a sense of belonging to something bigger than themselves, of inheriting ideas and values that must be protected and passed on intact.

Rituals set—and maintain—the tone and style of an organization. One stuffy, rank-conscious corporation maintains an elegant drinking club for its executives on the top floor of its skyscraper headquarters. Near the door is a table reserved, by Inner Face rule, for the dozen or so members of top management; no lesser mortal would dare sit down at it. But whenever an executive achieves some triumph he is well advised to repair to the drinking club at precisely 5 p.m. to collect his reward. There, with a great show of bonhomie, he is invited to join the big boys for a drink at the round table. Everyone present recognizes the accolade; the word goes quickly through the grapevine and Mr. Bright can bask in his new status and in the envy of his colleagues. The participants in this little game take it very seriously; it is a vital sacrament of the creed they work by, reminding them of who and where they are.

The basic conservatism that characterizes the Inner Face has been criticized by many writers. Keith Davis points out that informal groups "perpetuate cultural values which the group holds dear." And he goes on to say that "there develops a tendency to perpetuate the status quo and to stand like a rock in the face of change. What has been good is good and shall be good! If, for example, job A has always had more status than job B, it must continue to have more status and more pay, even though conditions have changed to make job A now inferior.... Although informal organizations are bound by no chart on the wall, they are bound by convention, custom, and culture."

A gyroscope resists change too, and in doing so provides the stability without which no orderly progress is possible. Humming quietly along in its own orbit, the Inner Face is like a gyroscope, keeping the organization on an even keel, protecting it from the effects of sudden squalls, resisting abrupt and impulsive changes in course. What is important to remember is that the human values the gyroscope maintains are values that the formal organization overlooks—or delegates to the Inner Face.

The seven members of the United States Board of Federal Tea Tasters sip judiciously at their annual meeting, as they have since 1897 despite all official efforts to get rid of them. When President Richard M. Nixon sought to abolish the board in 1970 as a waste of the taxpayers' money, the unofficial, informal structure of the organization—aided by tea-industry lobbyists and interested Congressmen—resisted. Eventually, Nixon gave up.

Life among the bureaucrats

The newly hired employee of any big (or even not so big) organization tends to arrive with a bad case of first-day-in-the-office shakes. For the portals close behind him like the jaws of a trap and there he is, alone and defenseless, not knowing the way to rest room or water cooler—or to success. He is awed by the sight of apparently well-adjusted veterans performing tasks he figures must be far beyond his talents. It will be only a matter of time, he is pretty sure, before his terrible inadequacies are discovered.

What may happen to him next is lampooned on these pages by cartoonist Robert Osborn, who has learned his own way through the mazes of big business organizations and can still sympathize with the hapless, disoriented newcomers who have not.

Things do get better—they could hardly get worse—as the outsider goes through the abrasive process of becoming an insider. Some of his new colleagues will show him the ropes, brief him on office protocol, clue him in to who are the good guys and the bad guys, steer him in the effective ways —whatever the organization manuals say—to get things done. His own adaptability will make him surer of himself. Almost before he realizes it, he is a veteran himself—and seems a formidable figure to the next newcomer who timidly enters the organization's door.

DRAWINGS BY
ROBERT OSBORN

The first-day syndrome
Reporting for work at the outset of his career with the organization, the new man is so filled with anxieties that if someone were suddenly to turn to him and bellow, "Go away!", he very well might.

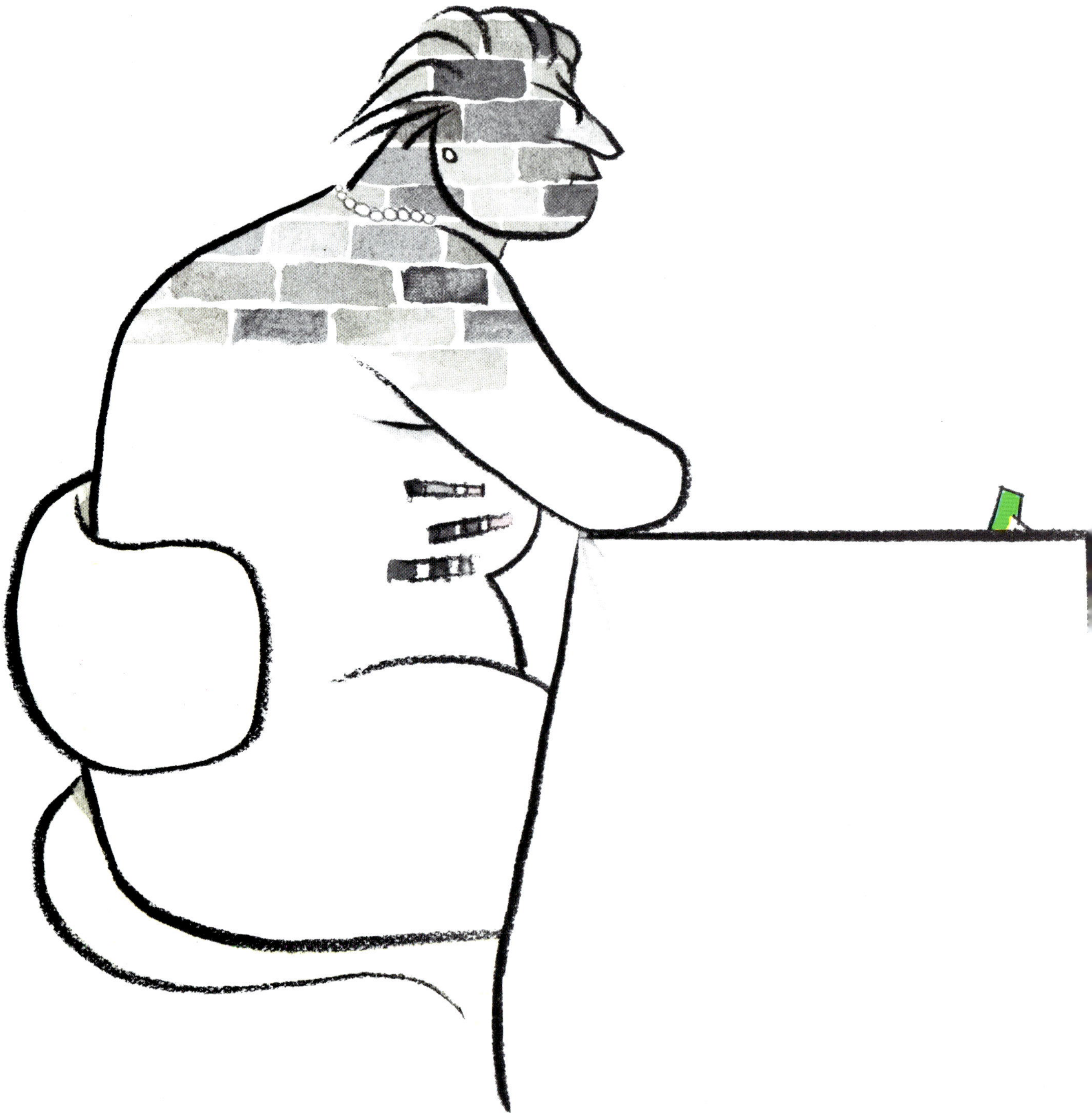

A pat on the back

A man who thinks he has outmaneuvered the secretary or another skilled office infighter should, before he prematurely takes a bow, look to see just what is sticking out through his shirt front.

The gatekeeper's unofficial clout

Stone walls may not a prison make, but if they are personified by the boss's protective secretary, it may take a good deal of guile for a supplicant to get around the barrier. And while the official corporate rank of such key individuals may be low, their potential for blocking careers may be quite devastating.

The communication center
The grapevine around the water cooler carries the news that really matters. That is still the place to find out who is building a meaningful relationship with whom, and whether the profit announced in the annual report is imaginative accounting or a signal to ask for a raise.

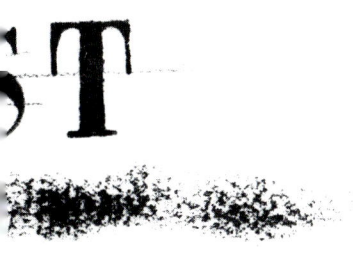

The two-way funnel

Not just an in-one-ear, out-the-other instrument, the double funnel is a key employee: He collects office gossip and reports it to the boss, and also spreads rumors inspired by the boss himself to test reaction within the organization.

Semivoluntary donations

Group loyalty is expressed, among other ways, by chipping in to buy gifts for employees who are going away, coming back, getting married, having a baby, transferring to another division or simply moving four doors down the hall.

Rising to the challenge
Onward and upward toward the heights streak the comers, not always by the methods Horatio Alger prescribed. Those who pause to look back seldom make it.

Group solidarity
Adjusting to his corporate niche, the employee dons a new identity while shedding his old one. In time he becomes so much a part of the organization that he helps sustain it while being sustained by it. By then, moving in lock step with his fellows is second nature to him.

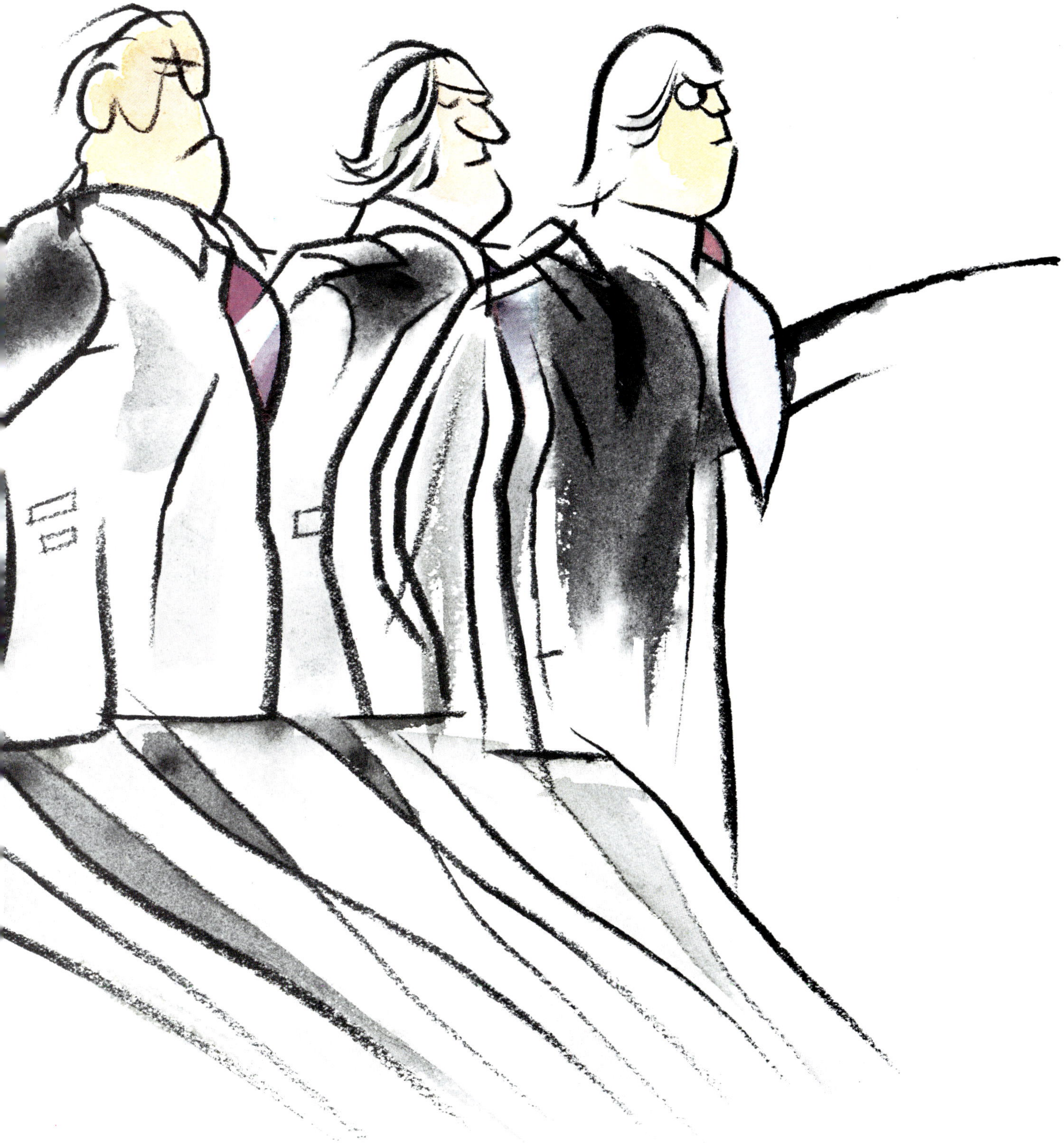

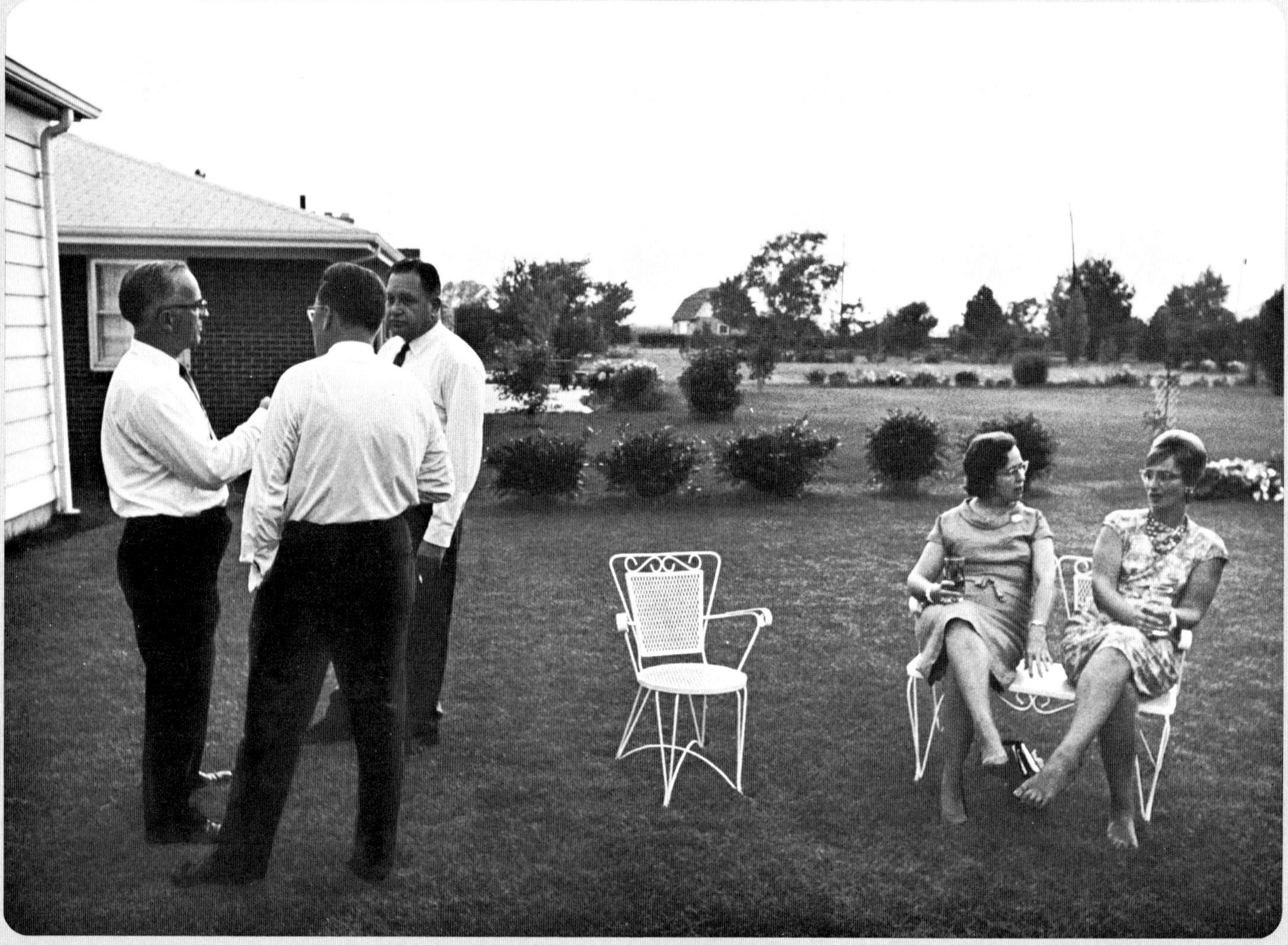

Strain on the Home

In the early 1820s the founders of the American textile industry set up company towns in New England and created a way of life for their employees that has rarely been duplicated in a free society. The millowners were firm in their Puritan belief that hard work was the path to salvation—a belief that also made good business sense—and they recruited thousands of young, unmarried women from the surrounding countryside to tend the looms from 5 a.m. to 7 p.m. six days a week.

To keep the devil at bay, the God-fearing entrepreneurs in Lowell, Massachusetts, took charge of the young ladies' remaining 10 hours a day as well. Under the "Lowell factory system," the women lived in company-owned, carefully supervised boardinghouses (where they were locked in at ten every night); company rules prohibited card playing and "ardent spirits," scheduled the start and finish of all meals to the minute, and dictated—at the pain of dismissal—that every employee attend church regularly and obey the "blue laws" on Sunday. The young women spent their scant leisure hours obediently improving their minds and souls; they studied Seneca, Newton and the Bible, formed an Improvement Circle and even founded the *Lowell Offering*, one of the first magazines exclusively for women.

Foreign visitors were shown Lowell as a model of Yankee progress, and they came away with mixed impressions. In 1834, French author Michael Chevalier wrote that "under this rigorous system there is a somber hue, an air of listlessness, thrown over society. . . . Lowell is not amusing, but it is neat and decent, peaceable and sage."

It was also short-lived. After a decade or so the millowners, pressed by falling prices, cut wages; and the young women of Lowell, clad in white muslin dresses, green stockings, and carrying green parasols, marched through the streets on strike. No longer was the Lowell factory system a social and economic success. By 1840, Orestes Brownson, a New England clergyman, observed that the young women of Lowell, instead of earning their hoped-for dowries, wore out "their health, spirits and morals" and were forced to "go home to die."

Except for monasteries and convents—and perhaps some large Japanese corporations *(pages 54-63)*—few organizations today match the Lowell mills' influence over their members' lives; even Army draftees are free to spend their off-duty hours as they wish. But everywhere the long arm of the organization still reaches deeply into most people's private and personal affairs.

Particularly since the Second World War, many a modern organization has become a tight little island of its own—a social and economic community with distinctive folkways, mores, values and loyalties to shape the lives of its employees. Large corporations have become enmeshed with all kinds of nonbusiness activities—company athletic teams, savings plans, retirement schemes, in-house psychiatrists—to emulate the influence over private life styles long exerted by military, church and academic institutions. Nearly all organizations, in fact, now determine a tone and a way of life that is far beyond the worker's immediate job or salary.

Even when no direct intervention in private affairs is intended, the organization has a heavy effect because, liked or disliked, it is the source of livelihood. It determines the quality of a member's home life and the happiness and mental health of his wife and children. When William G. Dyer, Professor of Organizational Behavior at Brigham Young University, studied the families of factory workers, he found that the man's job satisfaction—or lack of it—was the single most important factor "influencing the whole tenor of family life." In one family the wife said her husband's unhappiness with his work was the main domestic problem. She tried to persuade him to change jobs, but he was afraid that he could not find another that paid as well or was as steady as the one he had. The entire family, meanwhile, carried part of his misery. "Daddy is cranky all of the time," one child said. "He used to take us to the movies, but now he doesn't any more."

An organization touches the private lives of its members at many critical points. It can exert blatant control, as a corporation does when it suddenly transfers an employee from one part of the country to another, uprooting his entire family; more often the organization's influence is subtle, perhaps taking the form of unmistakable hints about where to play golf or what charities or political candidates to work for. The organization may also choose its members' friends and shape their social lives by determining what associations or clubs they should join. It may influence how they spend their weekends, the age at which they retire, the clothes they wear and the places where they take their vacations. (Some European companies provide vacation villas and rent-free apartments to their executives as "perks," extra perquisites of office in addition to salary.) In some instances, the organization may determine whether and whom they marry; in Japan, it may even serve as matchmaker —and then cater the wedding. In every country, organizations increasingly make the fundamental decision about where their members live.

Many commentators have discerned the doom of individual freedom in this influence. They warn that people who let an organization make all their decisions for them are heading for psychological trouble. In

The Organization Man, William H. Whyte Jr. pointed out that many organization families rely on pension plans, payroll deductions and profit sharing to take care of their futures, and consequently go into debt to finance purchases rather than saving for them in the old-fashioned way. "They don't trust themselves," he wrote, and beg for an "external discipline" such as the monthly payment book; "they want entrapment—constant entrapment"—for "our whole population is moving toward the more regularized life." George Labovitz, a professor of behavioral sciences at Boston University, adds, "Whether in the form of company bowling leagues, health plans, or an executive retreat, the trend seems to be toward a type of 'organizational feudalism,' in which the individual is completely dependent upon the organization for his financial security and the fulfillment of his social needs."

But most employees of large organizations take a quite different view. They do not see themselves as serfs entrapped in anybody's feudalism. Instead, they regard their benefits as part of their remuneration for services rendered, not as the organization's attempt to control their private existence. They enjoy living the organizational life. It provides the income, comfort, power and status that they crave, and if they have voluntarily relinquished some of their freedom to get such advantages they can always give up the benefits of the system and find some other way to earn their livelihood.

Within the United States, the organization's private influence seems to bear most heavily on the wife. To begin with, she often must meet stiff standards if her husband is to be hired—or get ahead. Some corporations still screen the wives of promising executives to make sure they will fit in with the institutional image. At the very least, such a test requires dinner with the boss and his wife, an uneasy occasion under any circumstances. According to one survey of 50 American companies, the wife's virtues are supposed to include cooperativeness, graciousness and the capacity to accommodate; intelligence is not considered important.

Many companies hire executive recruiters when searching for new talent. These "head hunters" often check on a candidate's wife. Russell Reynolds of New York says he always interviews the prospective executive and his wife. "Often the difference between two top men being chosen is whether the man has an outstanding wife," he says. The woman's role can be particularly important if her husband is posted as a regional representative of a large organization in a small town. "The man, and his wife, simply cannot divest themselves of corporate identification," says sociologist Wilbert Moore. "Their every activity with persons outside the immediate family is likely to be tinged with a recognition of the man's position. He represents the company willy-nilly. . . . Whether his wife is in a position to do him much good . . . she is clearly in a position to do him much harm. If she flouts local convention . . . the manager will be held to blame."

Chapter 5

But the chief problem facing the executive's wife is seldom her failure to satisfy some theoretical set of qualifications but rather simple loneliness —the aching frustration of being married to a man she rarely sees or talks to. She must suffer long separations from her husband while he works nights and weekends or travels on business. When he finally does stagger in the door with a briefcase full of papers, he often is so drained emotionally and physically that he has no patience or energy left for his spouse.

The wife's loneliness is not made any easier if she recognizes that her husband enjoys his total submersion. The fact is, of course, that many men dive into their work—and their organization—because they like it. William H. Whyte Jr. contends that the top executive drives himself "because his ego demands it . . . the theme is self-expression." Despite the long hours at the office, the hectic travel, the sleepless nights worrying about company problems, 90 per cent of the leading executives Whyte interviewed did not regard themselves as overworked. "Overwork, as I see it," said one company president, "is simply work that you don't like. But I dearly love this work." A clergyman in Bloomfield Hills, a suburb of Detroit where many top auto executives live, sees them as "monks who have

Homework, expected of organization men who hope to get ahead, could keep this accountant from sharing the busy family activities that surround him. His solution is to work in the kitchen.

traded in their prayer books for a production line. . . . I don't give as much of myself to my church as many of them do to General Motors and Ford and the rest." One woman in Bloomfield Hills reported that she and her husband had not been out after nine in the evening for six months. "He's away on business a lot and when he's home he leaves the house before seven and gets back to dinner exhausted. Then he goes to bed. For all he gets out of it we could be living in a cave."

The organization's insistence on long hours at work can be quite explicit. One American oil company used to boast openly that its rapid growth was not due to any excess of brain power in its executive suite but simply to the fact that its top men worked seven days a week. Many companies keep their executives' noses to the grindstone by having regular breakfast conferences; and of course when a high-ranking man from the head office visits one of his corporate outposts, his local minions are required to be on call around the clock. Some managing directors make a habit of phoning subordinates at home in the evening to check up on them "when their guard is down." One told Whyte: "You promote the guy who takes his problem home with him."

In addition to keeping the husband away from his wife, organizational life seems to be set up so that it goes out of its way to make him dissatisfied with her. It provides a supply of female competition and a grander life style than she has at home. The competition can be cruel. Robert Seidenberg, a New York professor of psychiatry and author of *Corporate Wives —Corporate Casualties?*, believes "Work is very sexy, and the people with whom one is working are the people who excite." In Seidenberg's view, at least, "a day spent launching a project or writing a paper or running a seminar is more likely to stimulate—intellectually and sexually—than an evening spent sharing TV or discussing the lawn problems or going over the kids' report cards." But whether work is sexy or not, modern organizations are full of young women. Middle-aged men, often for ego satisfaction, play up to them; and the more ambitious women actively seek the company of successful older men.

The organization not only provides sexual competition for the wife but it also frequently creates economic competition with expense accounts. The company pays for fancy lunches, dinners, jet flights and luxury hotels without their costing the husband a cent. If he spends much time traveling, he can soon grow accustomed to his steak and prime ribs and room service —while his wife is cooking hamburgers or chicken at home for herself and the children.

Sometimes, particularly in Europe, the wife also shares the luxuries of an organization-sponsored life style. European executives and their families are often subsidized in a private life style grander than that of their United States counterparts. Because income taxes are far steeper than those in the United States, European executives are paid lower taxable salaries but are given many easy-to-take—and tax-free—perks instead, including the private use of company cars, houses and vacation retreats. In France,

November 1959: *Taranto, Italy. While Dick worked on missile sites, the family lived in town. Mark, at far right with a delivery boy, learned Italian.*

June 1958: *Huntsville, Alabama. Training for his first job, Dick lived with Barbara and Mark in a trailer, then in a house where Scott was born.*

August 1961: *Izmir, Turkey. Barbara met these camels on an outing when she and the boys followed Dick to his next job. The Brinckerhoffs lived for nine months in a desert trailer park.*

September 1962: *Ann Arbor, Michigan. Dick switched jobs to work on small rockets, and the family leased a house with a yard where Scott, age three, rides his tricycle. When Dick was sent to Nebraska for nine months, they stayed behind so Mark could finish the second grade in one school.*

August 1963: *Santa Maria, California. Sent West to test rockets, Dick took the family. They lived in this house six months, then returned to Ann Arbor.*

A mobile family's corporate odyssey

The Brinckerhoffs settle down in Southfield.

One out of every four salaried employees of big American organizations is transferred at least once every three years. Richard Brinckerhoff, en route to becoming international automotive and industrial licensing director for the Bendix Corporation, was even more foot-loose. In 16 years he and his family *(left)* moved 11 times, keeping a pictorial record along the way. Unlike many who travel the transfer trail, they did so without serious mishap or regret.

Dick was planning to be an automotive engineer when he learned of job openings for aeronautical engineers to install overseas missile sites. "I jumped on the bandwagon," he says, "like a true gypsy." Accompanied by his wife Barbara and sons Scott and Mark, he went to Italy with 300 other employee families, among whom the Brinckerhoffs established a solid core of friends.

In the 1960s, the heyday of space and missile programs, Dick and other engineers from this group migrated from one job to another. To them, transferring was normal. "We would just pack our bags," Dick recalls, "and go to the next job site." Wherever the Brinckerhoffs moved, they found themselves liv-

April 1962: *Middletown, New York. The boys watch grandfather (left) boil maple syrup. Dick, on a trip, had left the family with his parents.*

July 1962: *Huntsville, Alabama, again. At work on the Saturn space program, Dick moved the family and new dog, Queenie, to this rented house.*

August 1964: *Cochituate, Massachusetts. Queenie romps in the backyard of a house the Brinckerhoffs rented 15 miles from Boston after Dick took a new job working on Minuteman missiles.*

December 1964: *Titusville, Florida. When Dick was invited back to the Saturn space program as chief test conductor, the family moved to the seventh rented house, where the boys enjoyed building and cavorting on a front-yard tree platform. Later, knowing they would be in Florida for a while, they bought their first home.*

August 1969: *Montville, New Jersey. Dick shifted to overseas marketing in New York City and bought a home 40 miles away, where Mark (left) enjoys his high school commencement. In June 1974 the company moved the Brinckerhoffs to its Michigan headquarters.*

ing among old friends. "It was like a fraternity," Barbara says. Through the ties of profession and organization, their life style had been formed.

Independent and adaptable, Barbara coped alone with leases and household crises. The boys also became seasoned travelers. "Because Dick and I were excited, the kids were, too," she says.

The last move may be as permanent as organizational life allows. With Dick in management, the family settled in their Southfield, Michigan, home. But, says Dick, "We'd sell it tomorrow for a good experience someplace else."

135

for example, the rising young executive may be picked up at home in the morning in a chauffeur-driven Peugeot, at company expense; as he rises in the company, he will be picked up in a larger, more expensive, Citroën. Half the middle-level executives in Germany are given cars as perks, while in Italy a company manager may receive a free Ferrari, an apartment and a virtually unlimited travel allowance. A Belgian executive would receive a car and membership in a luncheon club as his perks.

When the job requires a transfer from one location to another, the organizational pressures that have focused on the wife take a toll on the entire family. Most large corporations with many branch offices and varied interests consider it imperative that any executive being groomed for a top job acquire a firsthand knowledge of all its operations. In an extreme case, one Montgomery Ward manager moved 28 times in 26 years. And many people move frequently as they seek new challenges and new careers; one American family moved 11 times in 16 years as the husband worked as an aerospace engineer during the space age and then shifted to marketing *(pages 134-135)*. In Europe, thousands of workers and their families shift across national boundaries to follow jobs—Spanish and Portuguese going to France, Italians to Germany.

For many families a move is traumatic. Ari Kiev, Professor of Social Psychiatry at New York Hospital-Cornell Medical Center, who specializes in corporate behavior, likens it to mourning. "You are giving up routines, giving up love objects," he says, "and it can be a very devastating thing. . . . The very mundane areas of life are most affected. You can't get the same brand of coffee. The newspaper doesn't have the same columnists. The radio stations play a totally different kind of music. Many of the things we take for granted change."

One executive wife who had just moved to a New York suburb told interviewer Irene Backalenick that she "was absolutely grief-stricken to be torn away from my lifetime friends and familiar surroundings. I was in shock. People who move many times don't know what real friendships are." And the wife of a newly transplanted executive "really felt rejected" when she discovered "the doctors were booked solidly and taking no new patients, and even the vet said 'No new dogs.'"

Teenagers deeply involved with friends and cliques and neighborhood hangouts are especially vulnerable to transfer blues. If they have moved frequently they may withdraw from any kind of extracurricular activities and keep new friends at arm's length. It is as if, writes Alvin Toffler in *Future Shock*, they wanted "to avoid new human ties that might only have to be broken again before long—as if they wished, in short, to slow down the flow-through of people in their lives." Younger children, who do not understand the significance of "promotion" or "better opportunities" and realize only that they are being torn once more from home and friends, may react by staging temper tantrums—especially if their parents are also distressed by the move.

When a move forces a wife to do things on her own that she normally would share with her husband, the stress is multiplied. "I went to the closing of this house alone," recalled one young wife in White Plains, New York, "and I had to make decisions on building. Even when I could reach my husband on the phone he was just too busy. I resented it, and I would happily leave this house because it generates so much hostility in me." Another woman finding herself in similar circumstances says she "felt like a pioneer woman, trying to be mother and father to the children. The whole thing seemed so useless with him climbing the ladder while our family went down the drain."

One nonworking wife, on looking back at 14 company-dictated moves, says "If I had said that we can't move again, we would not have moved. I know that. But I could never bring myself to say 'this is as as far as we go.' The question was: Should I sacrifice myself and my children, or should I make life worse by living the rest of it with a man who doesn't like what he is doing?"

The burden of moving can bear most heavily on the family whose members have created effective lives of their own. Psychiatrist Seidenberg tells of one contented wife with two children whose life fell apart when her lawyer husband took a prestigious job in another city and moved the family. In her former home she made many friends and ascended the social ladder while her husband advanced in a successful career; she was president of the garden club, acted in amateur dramatics and was a leader in the Junior League. She and her husband made a romantic couple, attending country club dances and parties and entertaining frequently. But in the new city, while her husband "continued climbing she seemed to have lost her former zest. She tried to make the social contacts expected of her, but she was now new—low person on the totem pole. . . . Although she was accepted into the membership of various organizations, it was quite apparent to her that unlike his, her credentials were specious, that she would be tolerated, but would receive none of the adulation that she had known. . . . She now had little personal identity. All the parties that she had given, all the successful affairs that she had arranged were in no one's memory. These were all things that people had to experience and could not be told about. The 'credit' was now lost." Furthermore her children were almost grown and could do without her, and her husband and her parents, calling her selfish and spoiled for complaining about her husband's successful career, refused to concede that she had suffered a loss by the move. She started drinking, and tried and failed to return to the nursing career that she had abandoned at her husband's request. After a suicide attempt she separated from her husband.

This tragic case is fortunately exceptional. Hundreds of thousands of families are accepting transfers, adapting expertly and learning to like it. "It's been a fantastic experience," says an IBM wife who has moved nine times. "I love meeting new people. Constant change helps you see things differently, and you grow up, you learn more with each move."

"The people who've moved before," says Ari Kiev, "have developed a style, a set of routines, a pattern of functioning they can shift into and say, 'well it's time to move, everybody knows their assignment,' and they get moving; and I think this contributes to some of the high morale." Many families who know they are going to be moving a lot prepare long in advance: nonworking wives take up "transportable" hobbies, and children are encouraged to learn sports that are played anywhere, like tennis, instead of ice hockey, say, or surfing. A woman temporarily living in Connecticut, who has shuttled several times across the Atlantic, says: "When we make each move we put down roots as though we were going to be there forever. We join the church, the garden club, and act like people who are settled and stable."

Seidenberg concedes that most organization wives do not suffer the fate of the lawyer's wife. "The vast majority," he says, "have made adjustments and adaptations, displaying . . . remarkable elasticity and resilience. . . . Possibly the most noteworthy thing about corporate wives is not that some of them develop illnesses when uprooted but rather that the vast majority indeed retain the capacity to gain personal pleasure from the successes of other persons (their husbands and children) and do so with a great deal of competence and grace."

Seidenberg's optimism may seem dated. The idea that happy homemakers will find fulfillment in providing cozy nests wherever their husbands' jobs take them may be out of tune with times in which many middle-class women work. Some experts think the working wife can more easily adapt to a transfer. But at least a few women will object to having to give up a painfully won high-ranking position in one place to start all over somewhere else.

Blue-collar families do not face the same organization problems as often as white-collar families. Indeed, many still live in the same metropolitan areas, or even the same neighborhoods, where they grew up, and they often prefer to stay there. When Ford shut down a plant in Buffalo, for example, it offered to transfer the 1,100 workers there to a new plant in Lorraine, Ohio, and to give them similar jobs. Only 20 per cent moved, even though there was widespread unemployment in Buffalo at the time. The reason the others stayed behind, according to one sociological study: "A life pattern of stability."

The blue-collar family's sense of personal stability may also protect it against many kinds of organizational intrusion. They, unlike some high-powered occupants of executive suites, choose their own friends without much interference from above. One assembly-line worker in England said, "My mates never visit me and I wouldn't like to see them. We like to forget work as soon as we are outside the gates. We see enough of each other at work; we want new faces." Another added, "Once you leave work, forget it. When you clock out, clock out your mind." Only 10 per cent of blue-collar workers queried in one United States survey reported that their best friends worked with them.

continued on page 143

Attending formal lunches for visiting dignitaries is one of the many semiofficial tasks that Pat Cartwright performs in her role as the wife of Lieutenant Colonel Ian Cartwright (right).

Duties of the colonel's lady

A woman who marries an army officer is willy-nilly enlisted into service, too, and her nuptial vows may turn out to be almost an oath of office. Like many an organization wife, Patricia Cartwright, whose husband, Ian, commands the Third Battalion of the Royal Regiment of Fusiliers at Colchester Garrison in England, fills a semiofficial position that is essential to his career and to the organization he serves.

In Rudyard Kipling's day the colonel's lady—as the wife of a commanding officer—was often more to be feared than her husband was. Today the colonel's lady plays a less authoritarian role. Pat Cartwright sees her chief function as that of a go-between for the 250 families of men in her husband's battalion and the welfare services that the British Army provides—doctors, priests, social workers. She participates in volunteer organizations such as the thrift shop (*overleaf*), arranges such wives' club activities as fashion shows, and visits soldiers' wives at home and in the hospital.

In the best colonel's-lady tradition, she takes genuine interest in the welfare of the wives and children of her husband's men. As she explains, "We do try to think of the battalion as a family. Some people might laugh, but that is what we aim at."

Pat Cartwright takes her monthly turn as a volunteer in the thrift shop on the military post—sorting clothes, arranging displays, selling wares. Some profits finance children's play groups.

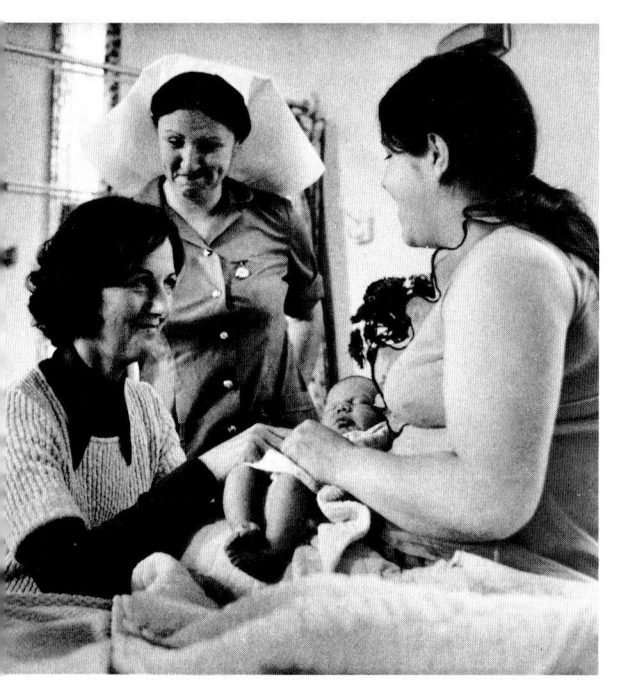

Visits to the military hospital are a ritual for Pat in her colonel's-lady role; she pays duty calls on all patients from the battalion, including this new mother.

Chance encounters with a social worker (seated right) and the Battalion Families Officer give Pat Cartwright a good opportunity to discuss their common concerns for dependents' welfare.

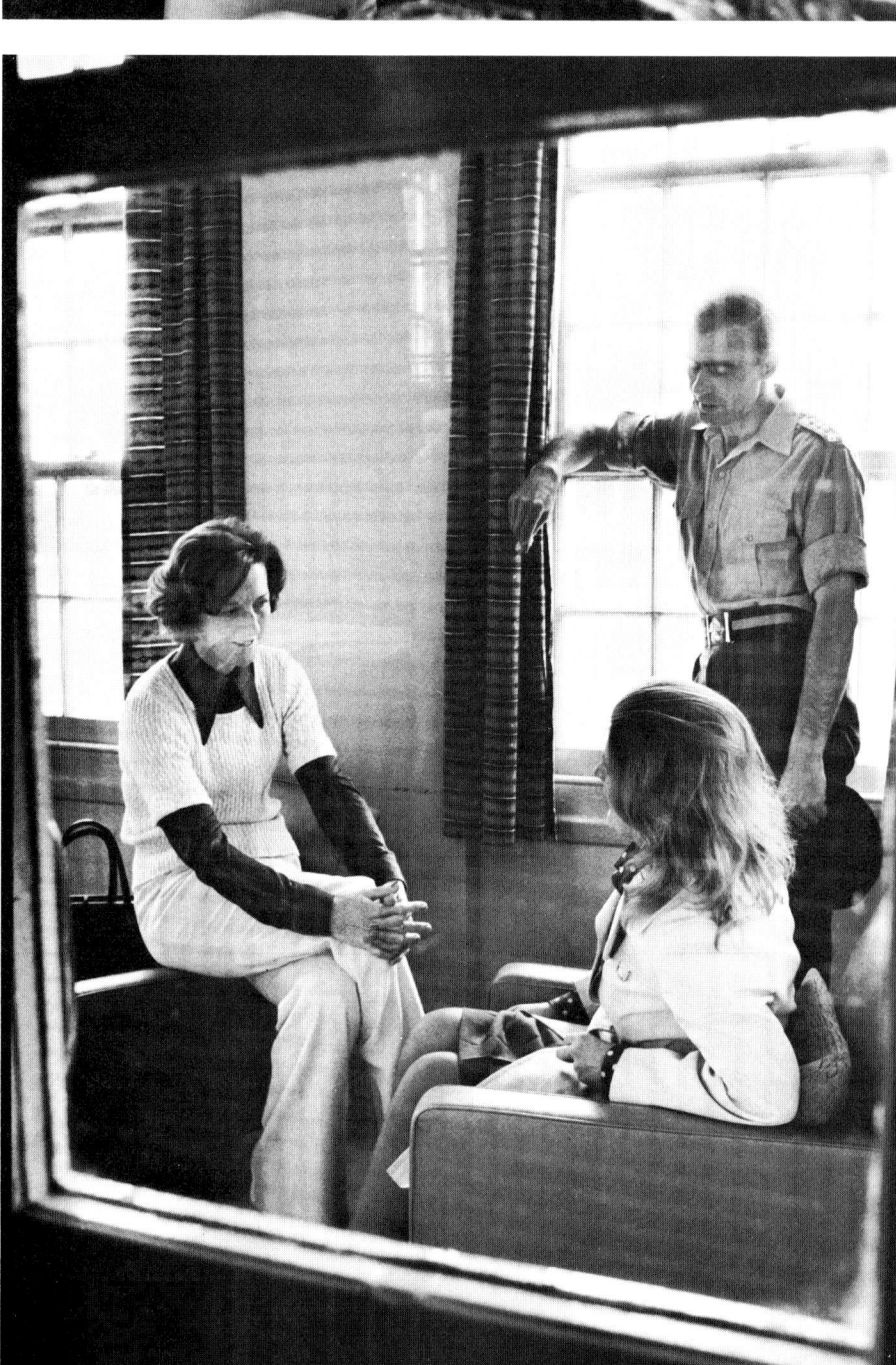

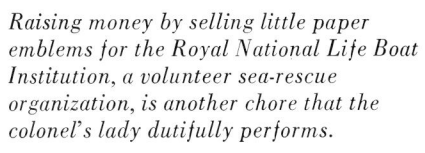

Raising money by selling little paper emblems for the Royal National Life Boat Institution, a volunteer sea-rescue organization, is another chore that the colonel's lady dutifully performs.

At the telephone center, where calls can be made to husbands overseas on active duty, Mrs. Cartwright (center, left) chats with other wives of British Army men.

While her husband serves in Cyprus on emergency duty, the colonel's lady carries on with only the telly and family terriers for company.

But even among blue-collar classes the higher the worker rises in the organization, the more closely his job determines who his friends are. A study of factory workers in the United States, Italy, Argentina and India reported that in all four countries skilled blue-collar workers make more social contacts on the job than unskilled workers. Because their jobs are more demanding, skilled workers enjoy talking shop with their peers. The higher their skills, the study found, the more the workers are required to move around and communicate with others to perform their jobs, and this mingling on the job leads to greater intimacy with various other members of the organization.

Most white-collar workers find their friends in the office crowd or among their suburban neighbors of similar professions and status. Many of them have no other ties; they have cut their roots from the neighborhood—and even the city—where they were raised. Their hometowns, class origins and backgrounds left behind, they seek new fellowships in their jobs, professions and acquired status levels. With each new promotion or transfer the process is repeated; they do the same thing one more time, perhaps adjusting the status of their new friends one notch upward.

For those on the way up the ladder, the organization can be quite cold-blooded about dictating a choice of friends. With no evidence of embarrassment, one business magazine offers the ambitious executive step-by-step instructions for breaking his ties to old friends who are now subordinates. He should find, it says, "logical excuses for not joining the group at coffee breaks or lunch." He should "miss the department bowling or card sessions, occasionally at first, then more frequently." If invited to the home of a subordinate he can go—at first—but he should not invite subordinates to his home unless he entertains a number of them at the same time. As he gradually severs all social relationships with erstwhile colleagues, his wife, he is warned, may resist, because she does not "understand the protocol.... A wife can be downright dangerous if she insists on keeping close friendships with the wives of her husband's subordinates. Her friendships will rub off on him, color his judgment about the people under him, jeopardize his job."

This process may even work in reverse. A rising executive may have to shun aristocratic acquaintances lest he give away his highborn status and offend organizational superiors who are socially his inferiors. One junior executive told William H. Whyte Jr.:

"Because of this last transfer I'm back here, almost by accident, where I was born. It ought to be a setup; frankly, my family is as old guard around here as they come. Well, it's a lot of crap, sure, but I must say I get a good bit of pleasure knowing I can join the City Club and my boss can't. But it's damned privately I think about it. If I am going to go ahead in this organization, the people I've got to get along with are the office crowd, and don't think I wouldn't get the business if they started reading about me in the social columns."

As the executive rises closer to the top of his organization, his circle of friends grows ever smaller. Middle-level executives have noncompany friends and even mix them with office colleagues at cocktail parties. But in the upper-middle-class suburbs across the United States—in Greenwich, Connecticut; Winnetka, Illinois; and Hillsborough, California—class lines can be rigidly drawn. Social life is largely confined to office contacts and members of the same country club—and the two groups generally overlap. In Bloomfield Hills, where Detroit's automobile executives live in opulent, tribal propinquity surrounded by aides, suppliers, lawyers, bankers and advertising men, friendships are sharply limited. There is some socializing between competitors, particularly at the Bloomfield Open Hunt, a family riding club. But, according to John DeLorean, former general manager of Chevrolet, General Motors executives tend to pal around together; when they are not playing golf with suppliers or dealers they make up foursomes among themselves at the Bloomfield Hills Country Club; few of them have close friends outside the company. Such corporate friendships, however, can evaporate quickly. When GM executive vice president Semon Knudsen left the company in 1968 to become president of Ford, he ceased to exist as far as his lifetime acquaintances at GM were concerned —even though his father had been president of the corporation.

And when a top executive retires, or leaves the business, his old friends may completely disappear from his life. After the late Harlow Curtice gave up the presidency of General Motors, he wandered about in search of simple conversation. The golf professional at the El Dorado Country Club in Palm Springs, where Curtice lived in winter, recalled that Curtice was "the loneliest human being who ever lived. He comes into my golf shop for a couple of hours every day and talks to me and my assistant about the automobile business. We don't know anything about the automobile business, but we listen to him. He just seems to want to talk so badly."

In addition to picking friends for a member, many companies help decide how he will spend his time with them. Large organizations everywhere provide courses, lectures, hikes and other extracurricular activities for their employees. In the United States at least 10,000 firms have some kind of after-hours activity, according to the National Industrial Recreation Association. Bell Telephone Laboratories of New Jersey, for example, offers an extensive after-hours smorgasbord to its 17,000 workers. Bell Labs sponsors 300 clubs in 65 activities from amateur radio to wine appreciation. There are 15 clubs devoted to athletics alone. The company provides the meeting rooms, pays such club costs as subscriptions to magazines and takes care of duplicating and distributing club information to members. Bell Labs also sponsors educational courses in technical subjects related to the company's work and in nontechnical subjects such as foreign languages, creative writing and psychology. In California, Kaiser Industries Corporation offers, among other courses, instruction in portrait painting and stock-market investment, while the Raytheon Company in Andover, Massachusetts, has a gymnasium and track.

Some after-hours activities are specially favored by large organizations,

To executives, golf is so much the organization man's pastime that they take the sport with them wherever they go. On this course outside Dhahran in Saudi Arabia, employees of the Arabian American Oil Company play on "browns" —sand greens kept smooth with oil, which is cheaper than water there.

and the employees who get ahead get the message early. Knitting *(page 112)* is seldom among the required avocations. "Helpful" leisure activities may vary with the region: sailing in the Boston area, for example, hunting in Oregon, deep-sea fishing in Florida. But golf has been smoothing the way for big business deals ever since 1901, when Charles M. Schwab, after a round of golf at the old St. Andrews course in New York, persuaded Andrew Carnegie to join J. P. Morgan in creating the U.S. Steel Corporation. The Japanese have enthusiastically adopted this Western business practice, and have built so many courses that they have threatened to overwhelm their landscape with *gorufu kogai*—or golf pollution; fully 10 per cent of the Japanese population play golf.

"Golf," as one corporate observer explains, "is unexcelled as a prelude to the establishment of a business friendship." No other method of making contact with a prospect, he says, comes close to the "relaxed relationship that is effortlessly developed during a single round of golf. However tense the actual play may be, golf, in its interludes and postludes, is a talkative, outgiving, hearty kind of game. It is almost impossible to conclude 18 holes of golf with a man and not be on a first-name basis with him." Accordingly, many corporations pay for golf club memberships of their key officers and encourage them to play regularly—with the right people.

Another required after-hours activity for some American employees is philanthropic or civic work. It demonstrates to the public how much the company and its leaders are doing for the community. But it also tests the abilities of the aspiring executive—and his desire to put in extra time in order to get ahead.

"Training for philanthropy is a very important part of the training in our bank," says one general manager. "It's our policy to drill into our men from the very beginning that they must take an interest in the community they're working in. Even if they're just a manager in a small town they must take an interest in the new hospital, or school, or whatever it is. We get reports each year on every clerk in every branch, and this shows whether they have taken an interest in their community affairs or not. They're reprimanded if they don't show this community interest.... We expect to see the result of it somewhere in our balance sheet!"

Self-serving interest in selfless causes appears to be a peculiarity of the American system. There are other national idiosyncracies in the gray areas between organizational and private lives, but none perhaps is so illuminating as the differences in the patterns of entertaining business associates. This activity varies sharply from the United States to Europe and again to Japan.

In America, an executive and his wife jointly are expected, if not required, to entertain business "friends" and contacts; the cost can be a tax-deductible expense. Such business entertaining is provided at home or in private country clubs; in large cities the expense-account wining and dining may take place in restaurants. The wife plays a key role. One study reported two thirds of the white-collar wives believed they could best help their husbands by "taking an interest in the husband's work and being a good hostess."

In Europe, government officials and businessmen keep the organization at arm's length from personal social activities. The French, for instance, rarely entertain members of their own company outside of business hours, and almost never at home. Clients may be taken to lunch, but in a restaurant. British executives also draw a clear line between office and private society, maintaining their closest friendships at their clubs or with other men who wear the old school tie. The reason seems to be that Western European upper classes are still tuned to aristocratic social principles; they do not invite a social inferior to their homes, or visit his, just because he happens to be a corporate equal or a good customer.

The Japanese also rarely mix business entertaining with their family life. They do not invite business associates to their homes, and almost never bring their wives along to corporate cocktail parties or receptions. When an American businessman in Japan tries to do things his way by inviting a Japanese colleague and his wife home for dinner, the Japanese will politely accept—and then will usually show up on the doorstep alone, bearing the news that his wife unfortunately has a cold.

But mixing business with pleasure—outside the home—is an old Japanese custom fully honored by modern Japanese organizations. The Japanese tax office allows corporations to deduct $5 billion annually for entertainment expenses, and Japan spends fully 1.5 per cent of its gross national product on corporate entertainment. Every white-collar employee gets his proportionate share of company-sponsored night life. Customers and clients are entertained regularly—and of course they must reciprocate. To clinch a deal, not only must the salesman and purchasing officer dine together, but almost every executive or junior manager who has anything to do with the transaction is also expected to demonstrate his sincerity by letting down his hair ("opening up his belly," the Japanese say) in an evening of carousal with his opposite number in the other firm. Entertainment within the company is nearly as frequent, and every manager takes his immediate subordinates out several times a year for a night on the town—at company expense.

Wives never attend these functions in Japan (not even if the guest is a foreigner who quaintly insists on bringing *his* wife along). Instead, feminine companionship is provided by women who are professionals at the task: geisha for the surviving members of the prewar generation of businessmen, elegant bar hostesses for middle management, and bawdy cabaret girls further down the line. Big corporations maintain charge accounts at the most popular cabarets, bars and geisha restaurants and often hire the women of these establishments to pour beer and smile daintily at company receptions. An estimated 85 per cent of the money pouring into the Ginza entertainment district every night is spent by the *shayozoku*, the "expense account tribe," who drop $500 million annually at the area's 1,000 bars and restaurants.

Needless to say, no one objects to the requirement that everyone participate in these organization frolics—except perhaps for the wife, whose sole function in it all is to have a hot dinner waiting for her man, regardless of how late he staggers home.

In such ways—soaking up the delights of the Ginza, raising money for the Red Cross, playing golf with the boss, moving the family across the country, working weekends at home—the private lives of organization men are sacrificed, to some degree, in the drive to get ahead. Many people enjoy the organization not only for the status and affluence that membership confers but for the identification they get with power and a larger entity. For them, any organizational intrusions on privacy are merely reminders of their citizenship. So many people nowadays belong to one organization or another that it is those outside who risk feeling lost. And it is the members of the biggest, most pervasive organizations (such as the huge multinational corporations) who derive tremendous pride from working for a company on which the sun never sets, and who feel secure in the knowledge that the company will take care of everything. "Who among us," psychiatrist Seidenberg asks, "is so well integrated . . . that he can do without the security that identification with power brings?"

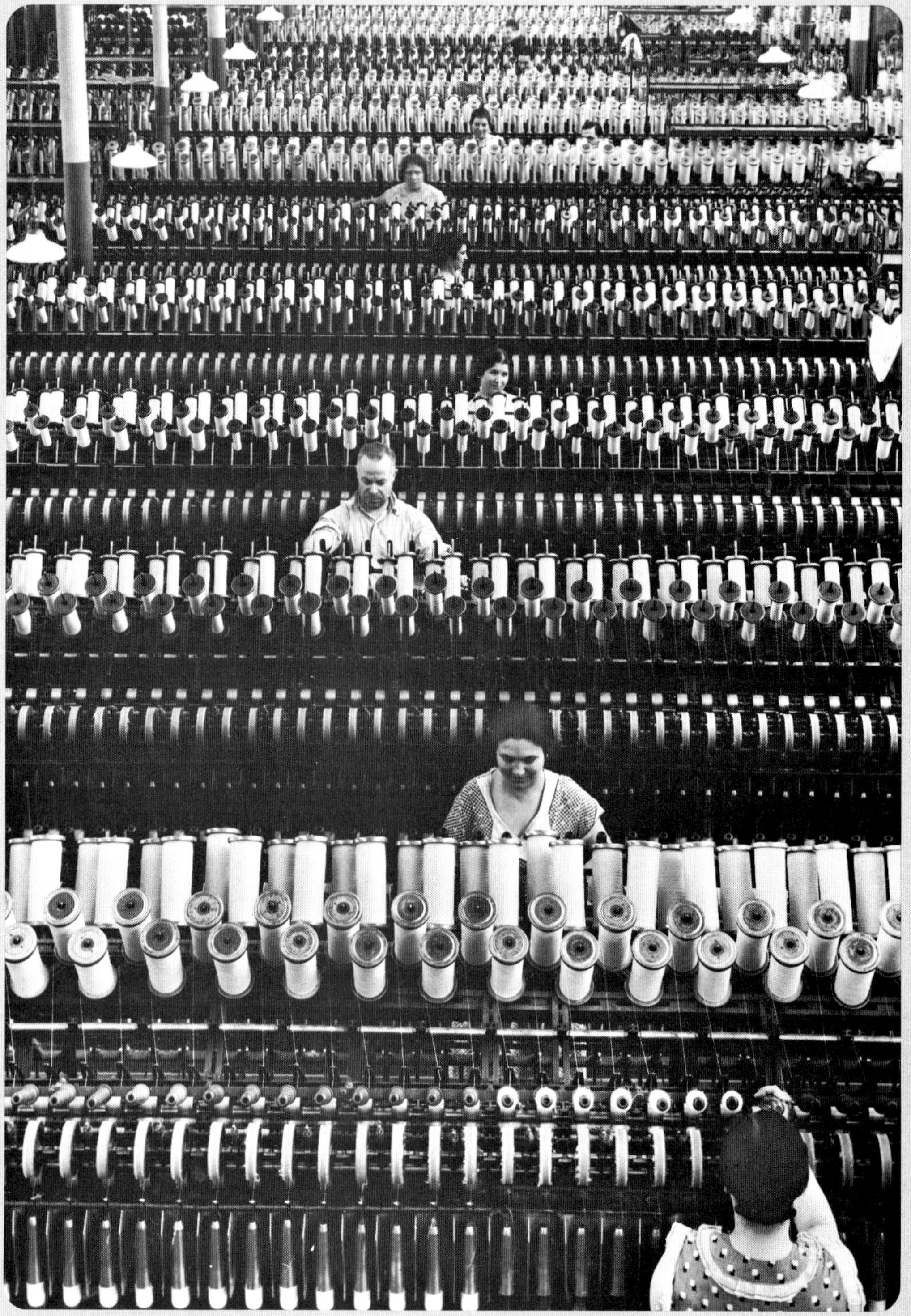

Challenging the System

6

To gather material for his book *Working*, author Studs Terkel asked 135 persons, from elevator operators to corporation presidents, "How do you like your job?" The overwhelming response was: "I don't."

A Chicago steelworker named Mike Lefevre explained the nature of the complaint simply and eloquently. "I would like to see a building, say the Empire State. I would like to see on one side of it a foot-wide strip from top to bottom with the name of every bricklayer, the name of every electrician, with all the names. So when a guy walked by, he could take his son and say, 'See, that's me over there on the forty-fifth floor. I put the steel beam in.' Picasso can point to a painting. What can I point to? A writer can point to a book. Everybody should have something to point to."

Like Mike Lefevre, few people in the modern industrialized world can point to a personal accomplishment in their jobs. A century ago Walt Whitman wrote that he could "hear America singing" at work, the mechanics and carpenters and woodcutters "singing what belongs to him or her and to none else." But today it is a rare and lucky man or woman who works at something that belongs to no one else. Most workers perform tasks just like thousands or millions of others, and there is no way at all for them to put their personal stamp on the finished product. If one of them were to disappear tonight someone else could pick up his tools in the morning, and with barely a flicker the factory or the office would turn out a product or service indistinguishable from yesterday's.

Such impersonal efficiency is a blessing of mass production and the division of labor in large organizations. In a material sense it has become a very real blessing to people everywhere. Since Whitman's day, the conditions of work throughout the industrialized world have improved dramatically. Hours are shorter, the purchasing power of a day's labor has increased greatly, machines have taken over much backbreaking physical toil and, despite inflation and recessions, most workers are more prosperous and secure than ever before. But for many people with nothing to point to, the job can be a curse. In fact, an exhaustive study prepared in 1972 for the U.S. Department of Health, Education and Welfare reported that "significant numbers of American workers are dissatisfied with the quality of their working lives."

In factories, in offices, even in executive suites, people complain ever more vociferously about their jobs—and their employers grumble that the "work ethic" is dead. In the American automobile industry, absenteeism doubled from the early 1960s to the early 1970s, to a rate of 5 per cent; it frequently soars to 15 per cent on Mondays and Fridays. In Italy, on some days, one out of every five workers fails to show up for his job, and there are plants in Sweden that have to keep one seventh of their labor force in reserve to make up for workers who stay home.

Such complaints are not truly universal. In the less highly developed countries, and presumably in China, the organizational life is looked upon as an ideal. And strangely, in one of the world's most highly industrialized countries, Japan, the organizational life is everyone's goal; the dissatisfaction that exists is fairly well concealed. But everywhere else, across the entire Western world and throughout the Soviet Union, there is a growing distaste for rigidly disciplined work.

In France, "the events of May" in 1968—riots involving students and workers seeking greater autonomy and participation in management—emphasized workers' bitterness. Says one French municipal official: "The cause of our most grave social conflict, a conflict which nobody discusses, is the refusal of young people to accept manual work." In the U.S.S.R., *Pravda* reported that "most" young Soviet citizens "felt that their lives were ruined if they had to become workers." Many large cities in the United States registered high unemployment rates in the early 1970s—while jobs as cab drivers, auto mechanics and domestic servants went begging. In industries almost everywhere, employees are declining to work overtime and are refusing to perform tasks they consider menial or degrading. An increasing number of labor disputes are concerned not with the traditional issues of hours and wages, but with the problem of job boredom.

European industrial and governmental leaders seem to have recognized the problem and to have taken serious steps to solve it before their American counterparts did. The late French President Georges Pompidou, commenting on a strike at the Renault automobile factory in 1973, remarked that "assembly line work that makes the working man and woman just a link in a chain" is becoming "less and less tolerable." As a result, some auto plants in Sweden have already done away with the assembly line, while workers elsewhere have been given greater responsibility for the finished product—and a greater variety of tasks to perform. German industry has operated for 20 years under a system by which workers' representatives sit on the boards of directors of large corporations, and workers in neighboring countries are negotiating for the same rights. More recently, American organizations have taken dramatic steps to humanize jobs and give individual workers more control over what they do and how they do it. Francis Blanchard, director-general of the International Labor Organization, declared at a Geneva conference in 1974 that "workers' reactions against depersonalized work could open a new chapter of contemporary social history."

If that chapter can already be seen in outline, it remains to be written out. In the meantime, many workers in all kinds of jobs are, to use a term heard more and more frequently, alienated from their work. Depending on who is using it, the word alienation can refer to a number of phenomena, not all of them bad. (An artist or writer whose alienation from the popular culture of his day impels him to create works that inspire later generations may be an example of useful alienation.) But people at work are alienated when they think they have nothing to point to, when they cannot see the connection between what they do and the final results of their work. Alienation strikes a worker when he is overcome by powerlessness, meaninglessness, isolation and self-estrangement. He feels trapped.

Men have labored at drudging, boring, unrewarding and apparently meaningless tasks for thousands of years. The advent of the Industrial Revolution more than 200 years ago took workers yet further from something they could point to. Critics have long been aware that William Blake's "dark satanic mills" can degrade the human spirit. In the 18th Century, Adam Smith, the intellectual father of laissez-faire capitalism, believed that the worker in the industrial system then emerging "generally becomes as stupid and ignorant as it is possible for a human creature to become." (Smith nevertheless admired the system because it produced more.) John Ruskin, the English author, noted:

"It is not, truly speaking, the labour that is divided; but the men—divided into mere segments of men—broken into small fragments and crumbs of life. . . . You are put to stern choice in this matter. You must either make a tool of the creature, or a man of him. You cannot make both. . . . It is not that men are ill fed, but that they have no pleasure in the work by which they make their bread, and therefore look to wealth as the only means of pleasure. It is not that men are pained by the scorn of the upper classes, but they cannot endure their own; for they feel that the kind of labour to which they are condemned is verily a degrading one, and makes them less than men."

Today, the outcry against alienation is intensified. One reason is simply that more and more people are caught up in huge organizations. In the middle of the last century fewer than half of all employed people in the United States worked for wages and salaries: 90 per cent did in 1970. In Germany, 85 per cent work for wages and salaries; in the United Kingdom, about 90 per cent. The concentration of employees into large corporations is so great that 2 per cent of the industrial establishments in the United States employ more than half the country's total civilian labor force. Within these giant organizations, job specialization may limit the individual to using only one or two skills out of all those he may possess; the organization's chain of command dominates his activities, controls his present and future, and tends to make him submissive and dependent. Moreover, the goals of the organization, and hence the ultimate result of the individual's efforts, are generally determined without his advice or consent.

A few experts have even concluded that these conditions of servitude are fit only for immature and even mentally retarded individuals—who perform better than normal people at many factory tasks, according to some evidence. But as one British industrial-relations expert commented, "the growth of affluence, the growth of education, has led to a shortage of morons," and consequently normal adults must fill these jobs.

One major cause of the deepening alienation has been the widespread application of the "scientific management" philosophy of Frederick Taylor, the time-study efficiency expert. He insisted that the work of management be divided up so that "each man, from the assistant superintendent down, shall have as few functions as possible to perform." Taylor's methods, which he promoted in the early 1900s, deliberately transferred all decision making and control from the workers' hands to management's brains and decreed that workers be forced to perform their tasks in the precise manner that time-and-motion-study specialists such as Frank and Lillian Gilbreth *(page 153)* set for them.

The demon of impersonal, mechanical efficiency still rules many organizations and harasses the lives of both blue-collar and white-collar workers. David Jenkins, who examined work environments in many countries, said in his book *Job Power* that Taylor-style management is "the most significant method of dehumanizing work ever devised." Franz Kafka once spoke with horror of how "the Taylorized life is a terrible curse, out of which only hunger and misery can grow."

Misery often enough did grow out of Taylorism, but his influence is only one factor in the increasing antipathy toward organizational life. Factory work, after all, was not slavery but relative freedom to men and women who had been breaking their backs picking other men's cotton or scrubbing other women's kitchens. The United States government report that described widespread worker discontent blamed it on "dull, repetitive, seemingly meaningless tasks, offering little challenge or autonomy," but added: "This is not so much because work itself has greatly changed; indeed, one of the main problems is that work has not changed fast enough to keep up with the rapid and widescale changes in worker attitudes, aspirations, and values." Between 1960 and 1969 the percentage of craftsmen and machine operators who had finished high school almost doubled, among both blacks and whites; yet the jobs remained the same and thus became less attractive for workers who had been given a tantalizing glimpse of a world of opportunity. The report concluded, "A general increase in their educational and economic status has placed many American workers in a position where having an interesting job is now as important as having a job that pays well."

The very concept of an interesting job has changed—and changed drastically. In the past, secretaries, clerks and bureaucrats considered themselves lucky that they did not have to "work with their hands." Their positions were hard to get and carried prestige; office workers felt close to decision makers. But today, as the government report points out, "the clerk, and not the operative on the assembly line, is the typical American work-

By analyzing his children's dishwashing and bedmaking chores, pioneer efficiency expert Frank Gilbreth, shown here with his wife and collaborator and 11 of their 12 youngsters, hit on principles whereby workers could eliminate waste motion. He was memorialized by two of the children in the 1949 book "Cheaper by the Dozen."

er." As the size of the office force has grown, white-collar workers have lost their elite status. To make things worse, white-collar workers, traditionally higher paid than the blue-collar class, have lost ground economically. In 1969 the average wage for clerical workers in the United States was $105 a week; the blue-collar worker was earning $130.

In a sense, white-collar workers, like their blue-collar counterparts, also are victims of technological change. The secretary who used to sit across the desk from her boss, sharing his correspondence, his trials and his hopes, now only hears from him when he hands her a recording to be transcribed; instead of sitting outside his office she may be down the hall in a steno pool. The bookkeeper, who used to do the company ledgers by hand, now is only one element in feeding information into a computer—and only the computer knows the true balance of the organization's books.

Many white-collar jobs demand a college education even though they offer no more pay, status or challenge than they did when a high school diploma was all that was needed to get one. One young Chicago woman, a recent college graduate, said: "I didn't go to school for four years to type. I'm bored, continuously humiliated. They sent me to Xerox school for three hours.... I realize that I sound cocky but after you've been in the academic world, after you've had your own class as a student teacher and made your own plans, and someone tries to teach you to push a button —you get pretty mad. They even gave me a gold-plated plaque to show I've learned how to use the machine."

To a surprising degree, even executives and managers are susceptible to the malaise of alienation. In 1973 a survey of 2,821 businessmen at all levels found that nearly half of them had changed—or considered changing—their line of work in the previous five years. In fact, 52 per cent of the supervisory managers, 40 per cent of the middle managers and even 27 per cent of the top-management executives were not satisfied with their jobs. These men were achieving success in terms of wealth, prestige and power, but they were discovering that they really wanted something else —although they could not always say what it was.

In recent years, thousands of executives in many kinds of businesses have abandoned the financial security and status of the organizational life for jobs that pay less but are rewarding in themselves. Some have become painters or singers, others work with their hands, a few start agricultural communes. The vice president of a New York advertising agency gave up everything to become a waiter in a ski resort. Very few of these corporate dropouts, according to a *Wall Street Journal* survey, admit to any regrets, despite financial difficulties: "Their disillusionment with their old way of life and work is so strong that it overrides any thought of turning back."

One executive who quit his job at a large oil corporation told a FORTUNE writer: "You felt like a small cog. Working there was dehumanizing, and the struggle to get to the top didn't seem worth it. They made no effort to encourage your participation. The decisions were made in those rooms with closed doors . . . the serious error they made with me was not giving me a glimpse of the big picture from time to time, so I could go back to my little detail, understanding how it related to the whole."

For William Clay Sargent, a 35-year-old vice president and shareholder of a major brokerage firm and a member of the New York Stock Exchange, the decision to quit was triggered by an ulcer. But the real reasons, he says, were "in my head" and were harder to cure. "Tentacles of responsibility were slowly strangling me and holding me in a job that would be my death. My job was in all ways unrewarding, except financially, and yet I could see no way out. . . . The major portion of my waking hours was spent in activities I felt were distasteful and deadening."

Many workers today—stockbrokers and steelworkers—complain about boring and meaningless jobs largely because they no longer suffer from the hunger and poverty that other generations had labored to overcome. The human spirit is so perverse that the fulfillment of one need does not make a person satisfied but triggers instead a new set of needs. A starving man will risk his life for food; once his stomach is full, he wants warmth and shelter. When he is protected from the elements he can think of safety, companionship and love; then he needs achievement, recognition, and finally creativity and self-fulfillment—the full expression of his potential.

This progression is the essence of the "hierarchy of needs," advanced by Brandeis University psychologist Abraham Maslow, a concept that underlies much thinking about organizational behavior. Maslow lists five levels of needs: physiological, security, social, ego and self-fulfillment, each of which remains dormant until the one beneath it is met. At each level the needs motivate behavior, but once a need has been satisfied it loses influence. If a person cannot breathe he will try to get air, but if there is plenty of air he will forget about that and move on to something else. A worker earning enough money to take care of his family comfortably, with his future seemingly secured by pension or some kind of employment guarantee, will no longer be content to work just for money. If the worker's social needs, at the next level, are satisfied by his neighbors, friends and informal work groups, still higher needs will assert themselves: his ego will demand knowledge, competence, independence, appreciation and respect, and finally he will look for self-fulfillment. These higher needs can be satisfied only by work that is "rewarding in itself," and that is rare in today's complex organizations.

Significantly, factory workers in underdeveloped countries, even those employed at the most boring and mindless assembly-line tasks, seldom complain about the nature of their jobs. They may strike often for more money, but they are content to work for utilitarian rewards, for they have only to look at their fellow countrymen to realize how lucky they are. They may not be hungry, but when they see the conditions of their nation as a whole they recognize that they are far from secure, and therefore they express few higher needs.

When the American or Western European worker looks around, however, his rising expectations are fueled not only by visions of unattainable abundance but, on television at least, by glimpses of higher values. His nose is rubbed in his own worthlessness. The television heroes are rarely factory workers or typists or clerks. Usually they are clever lawyers, doctors or news correspondents who disdain the routines of their jobs to follow individual, idiosyncratic pursuits.

On television, the United States government report pointed out, "Professionals lead lives of carefree leisure, interspersed with drama and excitement (never hard work), and . . . blue-collar workers are racist clods who use bad grammar and produce little of use for society." In real life professionals are often bored too—but at least they are not reminded of it by the mass media.

Many younger workers are also put off by time-honored practices at work. When three young men in their twenties were hired to clean offices at night they performed the task well. But one evening their foreman caught them sitting down on the job, reading and studying. When he gave them a

Chapter 6

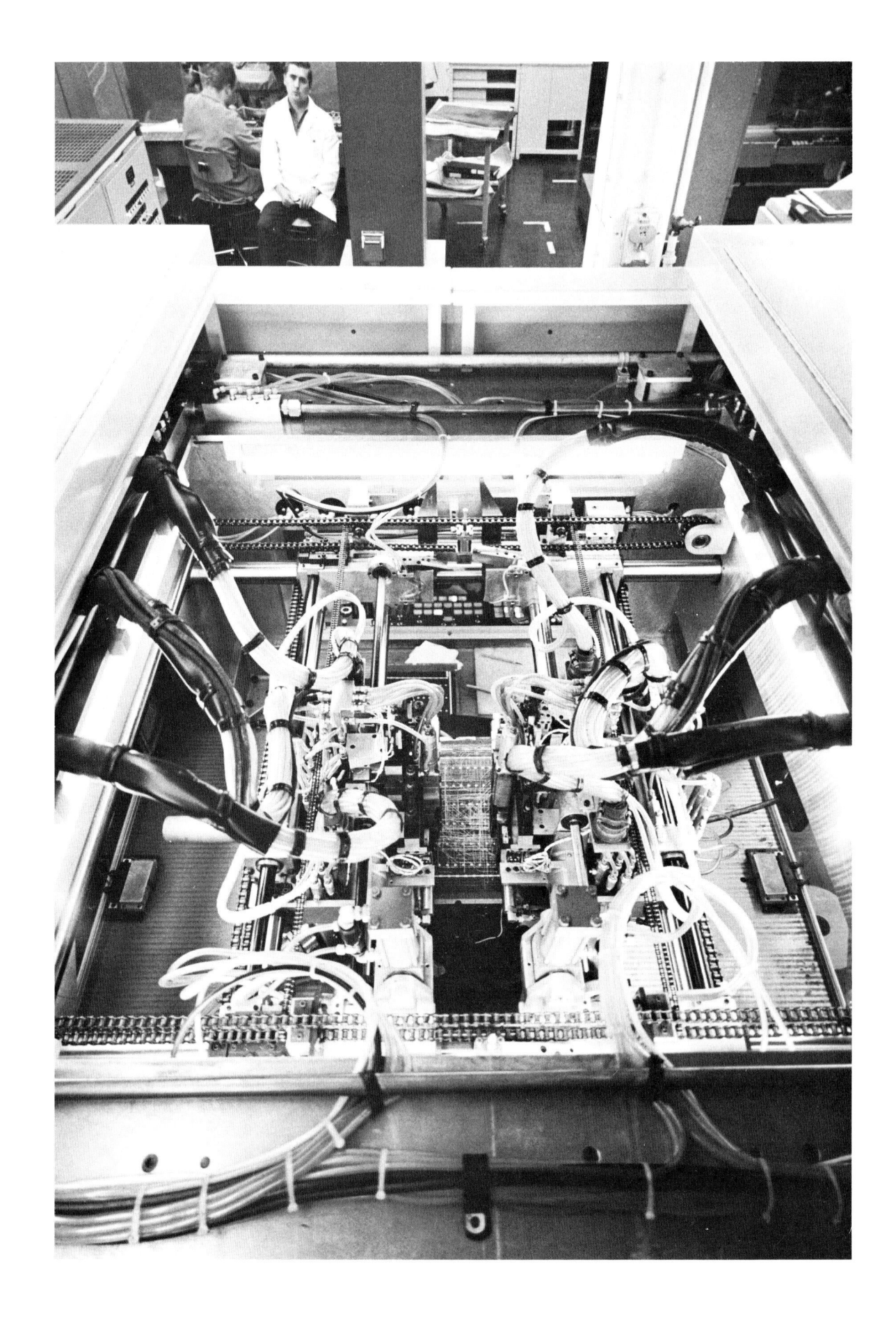

Baby-tending a machine, the young man at left epitomizes the worker trapped in a necessary but intrinsically boring job by narrow division of human effort into specialized roles. For eight hours a day at a German factory, he watches over the computerized machine in the foreground as it produces parts for still other computers. His main function is to alert a technician if he sees that any part of the apparatus is starting to malfunction.

written warning, the young janitors filed a union grievance: "We cleaned all the offices in five hours by really hustling, and who the hell should get upset because we then did our own thing?" One of them pointed out that "at school during study period I get my studies done in less than the hour and no one bugs me when I do other things for the rest of the time." The union steward had to agree with the foreman that the company "has the right to expect eight hours' work for eight hours' pay," and he "finally got the kids to understand by taking them outside and telling them that if they got the work finished in five hours, then the company would either give them more work or get rid of one of them." The grievance was settled by persuading the men to space out the work for eight hours.

All these causes of alienation—mindlessly boring tasks, affluence, rising expectations, changing values, annoyance with the rules of the system—can be discerned wherever human effort has been regularized by the organization. The dissatisfaction they bring is obvious to anyone who looks and listens in offices, stores, churches, military posts and factories. But the most dramatic manifestations of alienation break out on assembly lines, where workers ordinarily have nothing whatever to say about what they will do—or when they must do it. Nor do they receive the social support that flows naturally to other workers; informal work groups cannot be established on an assembly line because a worker can talk only with the people next to him; he may not know the name of the man two places away.

Furthermore, technology has not only failed to remove the drudgery from human work, but instead seems to have taken out much of the human skill. In many factories automated machines now perform skilled jobs like machining or welding, leaving the menial tasks for their human servants. A visitor to a modern auto plant will be impressed by great robots that take a rough casting and quickly perform dozens of drilling and turning operations to produce nearly finished engine parts. If the visitor looks around he will also see human workers; they are pushing dollies of heavy parts from machine to machine. British industrial engineer D.T.N. Williamson cites one factory that decided to automate the production of a clock, and accordingly broke down the assembly procedure into many tiny individual steps that machines could handle. But then the factory's engineers discovered that the steps were too simple and that human hands could perform the simplified operations more cheaply. So young women were assigned to carry out a series of minute, repetitive, boring tasks that were designed for machines. The humans got the drudgery.

The "blue-collar blues" infect production workers because their jobs offer little chance of advancement, and the men know it. A few might get to be foremen or rise in the union hierarchy, but they are well aware that plant managers come from business or engineering schools, not from the factory floor. There is also little opportunity for workers to quit their jobs and go into business for themselves, for the ever-growing conglomerates and the chains are steadily eliminating the independent small businessman. The despair of knowing they cannot escape from their day-

Chapter 6

Assembly-line workers put together Model T Fords as the conveyor belt slowly carries the chassis along past their stations. Introduced in 1914, this system revolutionized industry, produced a car in one and a half hours (instead of twelve and a half), reduced prices—and dehumanized the worker's role almost to that of an automaton. In place of the all-round craftsman stationed in one spot who made something virtually by himself, unskilled men were hired, trained to do one task and put on the assembly line to perform it over and over again.

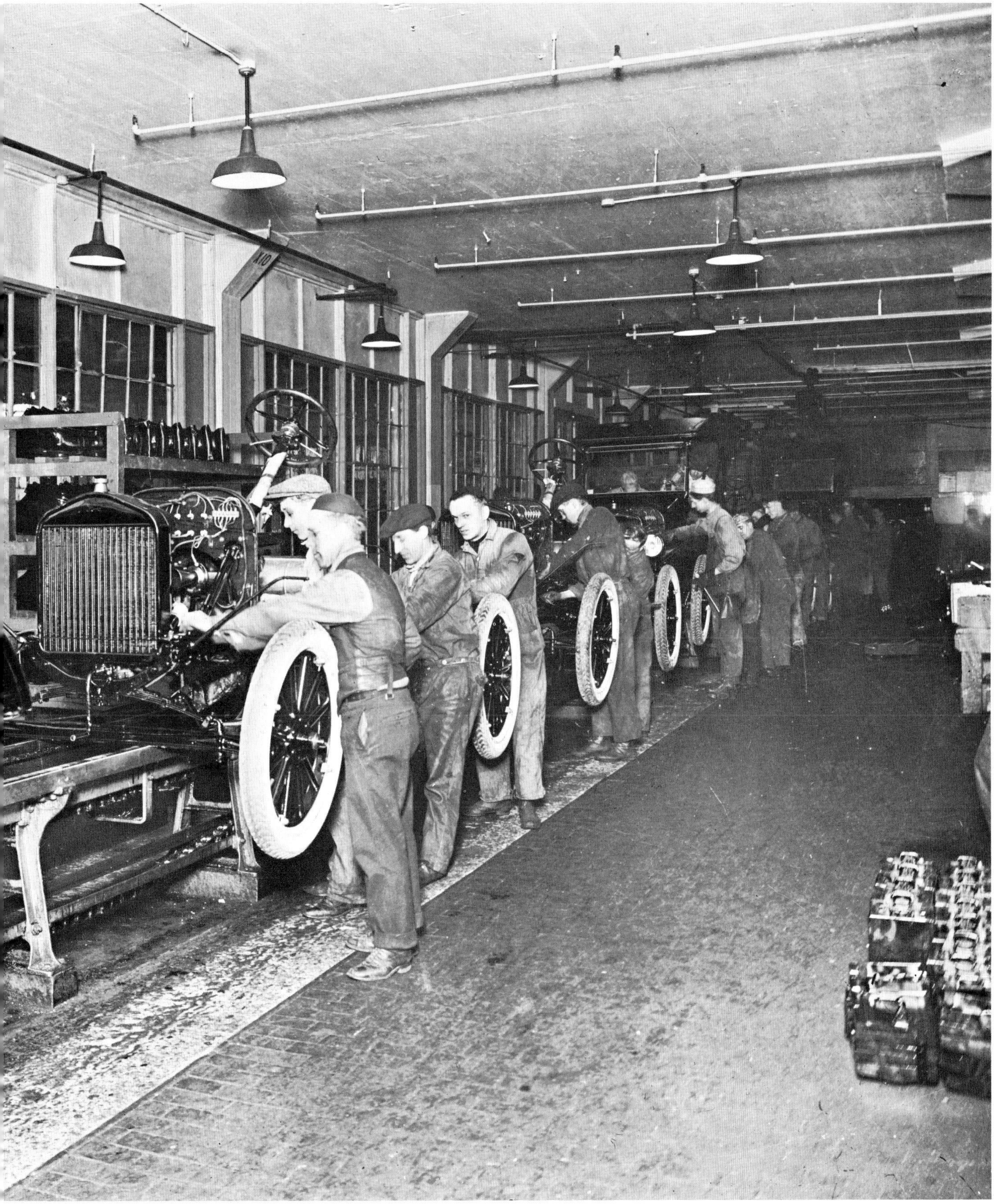

to-day frustrations is a potent ingredient of many workers' alienation.

All these currents converged in 1970 in Lordstown, Ohio, where General Motors had set up what was widely publicized as the fastest, most automated, most modern assembly line in the world. Capable of producing 101 Chevrolet Vegas an hour (compared to an average of 60 cars an hour in most American auto plants), the Lordstown factory was programed to cut 10 per cent off the normal labor costs of producing a car. The line had been designed by computer, with the time allotted for every job honed to split-second precision. (The time allotted to drive a screw, for instance, was computed by figuring the length of the screw, the number of turns and the speed of the power tool in the worker's hand.) The line itself ran at different heights so that workers would not waste a second bending or stooping. Most of the welding on the cars was performed by robots, called Unimates, which never get bored or tired, of course, but must be assisted by unskilled human laborers who do. When the plant opened, one auto-industry executive called it "the wave of the future."

But if Lordstown influences the future it will be as the symbol of alienation and of revolt—not as the prototype of 21st Century efficiency. To produce 101 cars an hour, the 8,000 young Lordstown workers had to repeat exactly the same tasks every 36 seconds. And that may be just too fast. Trouble started almost from the beginning, and it intensified when the company laid off some workers and assigned their jobs to others. The resulting protests were less the classical union complaint against the loss of several hundred jobs than a rebellion against the crowding of one more chore into an already arduous 36 seconds.

And rebellion it was. "They tell you 'put in 10 screws' and you do it," a worker related. "Then a couple of weeks later they say 'put in 15' and next they say, 'well, we don't need you, give it to the next man.' " Some workers, to the consternation of executives, refused to do the extra work, and cars went by them with parts loose or missing. Cars came off the line with dents and scratches, slit upholstery and snipped wires. "They couldn't care less if the screw goes in the wrong place," a union official recalled. "Sometimes it helps break the monotony if the screw strips." At one point the Lordstown repair lot was jammed with 2,000 defective Vegas.

Management charged sabotage—and no one denied it. "Sabotage?" asked one Lordstown worker, "Just a way of letting off steam. You can't keep up with the car so you scratch it on the way past. I once saw a hillbilly drop an ignition key down the gas tank. Last week I watched a guy light a glove and lock it in the trunk. We all waited to see how far down the line they'd discover it."

The revolt climaxed in a 22-day strike that cost General Motors some $150 million, more, in the view of some outside observers, than the company had saved with the automated efficiency. Eventually management agreed to take back the laid-off workers and ease the work load. The slightly mollified workers went back to the plant, where the basic problems, of course, remained unsolved.

Perhaps the most famous of all protests against "the system" was Charlie Chaplin's classic film of 1936, "Modern Times." In this scene, Chaplin turns manic while tightening bolts on a conveyor belt's giant cog wheel—an idea that came to him, he said, after he heard about "industry luring healthy young men off the farms who, after four or five years at the belt system, became nervous wrecks."

The costs of alienation are enormous, and encompass far more than the dollars lost during a strike or cars damaged by sabotage on an assembly line. One cost is sheer escapism. Thousands and thousands of workers —on assembly lines and in executive suites—daydream through their work, paying enough attention to get the job done but little more. A 1972 Gallup Poll revealed that 57 per cent of all American workers—and a massive 70 per cent of the businessmen and professionals interviewed —thought they could produce much more each day if they wanted to. Many said they were only working at half their potential—but that was all the job required. Others escape through alcohol and drugs. Accounts of three-martini, expense-account lunches are legion—and true. In some factories, workers stay high on drugs throughout their entire shift. In 1972 the United Automobile Workers conducted a survey of one plant with 3,400 workers to measure how many were taking drugs—and found that 15 per cent were on heroin. Alienation affects health in less dramatic ways too. Studies by the University of Michigan's Institute for Social Research found that job satisfaction is directly related to mental health—and that diminished job autonomy, isolation and technological change lead to psychosomatic illness, anxiety, worry and tension.

Another cost of alienation is the loss of commitment and loyalty, two virtues that appear to be dwindling. "Loyalty?" says a New York bank employee, "That's kind of archaic. It's really if you like your job, if it's what you need and what you want. The job is not loyal to you." A corporate consultant with more than a touch of cynicism told Studs Terkel: "The only loyal people are the people who can't get a job anyplace else."

Chapter 6

Organization rules do not invariably, but only generally, prevail over desires of the individual. The Dutch soldier at far left, member of an honor guard at The Hague, gets away with wearing his hair shoulder length because Army regulations concerning hair and haircuts have been abandoned. Ironically, it was another large organization that gained this acceptance for individuality: a soldiers' union to which half the Army's 60,000 men belonged won the rule relaxation in 1971.

That may be too cynical a view, yet the great cost of alienation is undeniable, not only in commitment and loyalty, but also in wasted money, inefficiency, illness and the crushing of the human spirit. The causes are understandable, and so are the reasons they do not apply with much force in some underdeveloped countries. But Japan? Why, in a country where most people are exceptionally well educated, affluent, ambitious and forward looking, does the organizational life seem to be so much more satisfying? The answer seems to be a spirit that imbues the Japanese organization, one that is not easily exported to other countries.

The Japanese worker is unusually devoted to his firm partly because of the knowledge that his job is for keeps, and partly from the company songs, badges and organized togetherness that inspire him. But equally important is the Japanese practice of continually training and retraining almost all workers to equip them for technological change and to assure that they never get into a rut. Long after Western training would end, the Japanese worker is still perfecting the skills of his own job while simultaneously learning many other jobs on his level. This training is at company expense and often on company time. Even workers who do not get promoted over the years become more valuable to the company, thus earning their seniority pay and enhancing their own sense of worth.

In addition, white-collar employees of a large Japanese corporation can always get advice on any job problem from their corporate *sempai*, literally, "the person whose footsteps he is following." Typically, the *sempai* is a senior officer of the firm, from the same town or university as the worker; he probably "introduced" the worker to the company in the first place and forever afterward functions as a corporate godfather and confidant. Never a direct superior, but on close and equal terms with those who are, the *sempai* keeps a close watch on his protégé's career, learns his problems and desires, administers semiformal praise and criticism, and supports him in the company. The *sempai* are always consulted when top management is deciding whom to groom for future leadership. If the Japanese corporation is like a family, as Japanese sociologist Chie Nakane believes, then the role of the *sempai* is that of favorite uncle.

But European and American organizations are not at all like families. An employee who stays in the same organization for life is increasingly rare, and without permanent employment neither the *sempai* system nor continuous training makes much sense. Clearly, the ideal of loyalty is not a practical solution to the problem of alienation in the West.

The human relations movement, which grew out of Elton Mayo's Hawthorne experiments in the late 1920s, nibbled around the edges of the problem; it emphasized motivation theories, the carrot as opposed to Frederick Taylor's stick. Managers were urged to pay more attention to their workers' human and social needs, to treat them with more respect, and to make them "happy." (United States Secretary of Labor Peter Brennan may have been only half kidding when he once suggested that corporations ought to bring go-go girls into factories to reduce boredom.) Planners, recognizing the importance of informal work groups, set up many kinds of councils and teams and forms of "participatory management" to tell workers about the reasons for decisions and to elicit their opinions. Although some of these techniques were temporarily effective, most of them eventually failed to motivate workers—as today's rising discontent demonstrates. Their failure led, for a time, to the sensitivity-training movement—also known as "T" (for Training) Groups—which attempted to bring out managers' "true" feelings toward their peers and their employees. Frequently the managers' failure to understand their own prejudices and inner needs had made it impossible for the techniques of "interpersonal relations" to work.

The trouble with most of these theories is that they were little more than psychological tricks designed to manipulate a worker's behavior without really getting at his inner needs. "Good management," wrote Walter R. Nord, a professor of organizational behavior, "is that which leads to the desired behavior by organizational members." "Participation" often meant merely giving a worker a sense of achievement where no real achievement was possible. Managers and foremen listened—but most of the time they did not hear what their workers were saying. Businessmen who gathered in management-improvement sessions to learn how to communicate with their employees were told by at least one expert that "the purpose of communication is persuasion." Many workers were not impressed.

Nowadays most organizational theorists realize that no amount of psychological tinkering can motivate a person to put his heart into a job that bores or degrades him. In the late 1960s, when this realization spread, the first genuine attack on work alienation began.

The new strategies seem revolutionary, for they assail some of the fundamental principles of modern complex organizations, including job specialization and the assembly line. Perhaps the most basic strategy is "job enrichment," which gives each worker more varied tasks to perform plus a greater degree of responsibility for the finished product. At the Corning Glass Company, for example, women workers used to produce electric hot plates on an assembly line, each person making one part of the plate over and over again. Now each worker assembles an entire plate and puts her initials on it for reference in case of flaws. The women schedule their own work flow and conduct their own quality checks. Six months after the change, rejects dropped from 23 per cent to 1 per cent, absenteeism dropped from 8 per cent to 1 per cent, and productivity almost doubled.

In a similar experiment, Motorola Corporation redesigned a production line to let each worker put together an electronic device of 80 different components instead of just working on one or two parts. This change cost the company quite a bit in additional training and manpower; it was not "efficient." But the extra expense was offset by higher productivity, better quality, lower repair costs and reduced turnover and absenteeism.

Job enrichment pays off in the white-collar world as well. Frederick Herzberg, a professor of management at the University of Utah and one of the leading work psychologists in the United States, describes one cor-

continued on page 169

To create an atmosphere of many small workshops, Volvo's Kalmar plant has been divided into areas, each occupied by one assembly team like the group above. The car body this team is about to work on has been turned on its side in order to make the undercarriage easier to get at.

Humanizing the assembly line

Disillusion with the organization life has been excessive in the automobile industry, where assembly-line operation also happens to be most highly developed. The boredom inherent in such repetitious work has been blamed for a high rate of absenteeism and employee turnover, strikes, even sabotage. In 1974, one Swedish auto maker, Volvo, risked a radical attempt to eliminate the impersonal nature of the work and set out to humanize the assembly line.

When a new plant was opened at Kalmar on the Baltic, the traditional assembly line was replaced with 18-foot-long, battery-powered and computer-guided moving platforms. The platforms are mobile work sites that glide silently around the floor, bearing car bodies to 25 work teams. Each team became responsible for one phase of production, such as installing the electrical system or assembling the body *(above)*. Every team member could do any other member's work, so they exchanged jobs at will. Each team also set its own work pace. The only requirement was a quota of about 13.7 systems installed for every working hour. The plant cost about 10 per cent more than a conventional one would have, but Volvo expects to gain increased productivity. A worker agrees: "It looks like a paradise, but we work hard."

Members of a Volvo team board a carrier to install electrical parts. Instead of each repeating one operation, they share tasks. After they finish, quality-control inspectors check on the team's work.

To provide the flexibility that permits each team to follow its own schedule, a worker in a control center mans a computer keeping track of the mobile platforms. Any platform can be stopped without slowing up overall production.

A troubleshooter, ready to help where needed, bicycles between partly assembled cars on their work platforms. The man at right is heading for a production-control television screen.

Workers on a Volvo assembly team gather for a coffee break in a carpeted private lounge. It was set aside just for them as a step in building team loyalty and humanizing their work.

poration where women answering mail from stockholders were made personally responsible for the accuracy and quality of their letters; instead of following established standard forms, they were encouraged to reply in a more personalized way. The outgoing letters were signed by the women themselves and were sent directly to the mailroom, rather than being routed to supervisors for checking and signature. In addition, each woman was assigned a specialty so that she could assist her colleagues in troublesome cases; previously, only the supervisor had been permitted to answer difficult letters. After six months the women with greater responsibility were clearly outperforming a control group; they were happier about their jobs and were absent less often.

Workers in many fields have responded to new challenges. British laboratory technicians at Imperial Chemical Industries Limited have been empowered to write the final reports for their research projects (a chore previously performed by their scientist superiors), and are held responsible for them. In addition, a group of Imperial salesmen were relieved of the requirement that they report on every customer call, and were told only to pass on information they thought someone else needed. They were permitted to make their own schedules, to grant some leeway in prices, and to offer immediate adjustments and refunds at their own discretion. Sales increased 19 per cent. In St. Louis, American Airlines gave boarding agents the responsibility for getting planes loaded and into the air. This experiment produced greater productivity—and some unanticipated benefits. One agent who nervously held a plane five minutes to accommodate 20 passengers from the canceled flight of a competing airline was complimented for his decision: the extra fares had more than made up for the cost of the delay. "I have more confidence in myself now that I see the confidence management has in me," he said.

Not all alienation problems can be solved, of course, by giving more authority to a single person. Where the task is too large for one individual to finish in a reasonable time, the new strategy calls on a production method pioneered in 1972 by Saab, the Swedish auto company. Saab eliminated a production line and assigned teams of four workers each the job of assembling 90 parts into four complete engines every 30 minutes—and then permitted the teams to determine their own procedures. Now each worker may build a complete engine by himself in 30 minutes, or all four can work on the same engine together, rotating specific tasks if they like, or they can divide up in pairs to produce an engine every 15 minutes. A team may speed up for a while and then take it easy—so long as it turns out eight engines an hour.

The Saab experiment was an immediate success. In fact, in 1974 Saab's competitor Volvo opened a new factory that has no conventional assembly line at all, but employs car-carriers on which teams of workers produce separate sections of the car, such as the electrical system, underbody fittings or the upholstery *(pages 165-168)*. The Volvo workers can slice up the job any way they please, so each person performs either one or several of the team's tasks, learns many skills and rotates in and out of hard jobs.

The team approach, coupled with a complicated system of "industrial democracy," has been embraced by workers, unions and management at another Swedish corporation, Gränges AE. At one of Gränges' small foundries, the team strategy increased productivity by 45 per cent, reduced turnover from 46 to 18 per cent, and cut spoilage by one third. At a larger Gränges plant, a 3,000-employee steel mill, one member of a melting team said: "Everything has changed since I've been here. Now we control the whole job. There is a foreman, sure, but he's busy taking care of materials and administration. He doesn't have to come around every five minutes and tell you what to do. Quality is very important here. If the rolling mill tells us something is wrong, we check into it ourselves. We don't need a foreman; we work together."

The assembly line has not been eliminated at IBM's huge typewriter factory in Amsterdam—but it has been humanized. In the past, IBM traditionally increased production by lengthening the line, simplifying procedures and adding employees—until the conveyor belt went on and on for more than 200 yards. In 1971, however, the company divided the plant into nine "mini-lines," each employing a team of about 20 workers and producing a complete component. As in Sweden, the teams apportion their own work, set their pace and take responsibility for the finished product. A few months after the change-over, production and quality rose sharply—while overtime, absenteeism and turnover declined.

The key to such experiments is to give workers more responsibility, and then to hold them accountable for the results. The Eaton Corporation plant in Cleveland gave its janitors control over their own supply inventories—and the job started attracting men who were interested in doing it well. Texas Instruments Corporation in Dallas reorganized its 120 janitors into 19-man teams, allowing each team to plan and schedule the cleaning of its area. Job turnover dropped from 100 per cent every three months to 10 per cent, and fewer workers were needed to do the job.

In 1971, the General Foods Corporation combined all the new techniques in a bold assault on work alienation. It built a new pet-food plant in Topeka with no time clocks and no status symbols such as executive dining rooms, parking lots or special carpets. Even the layout of the plant was designed to encourage informal gatherings during working hours. In this factory, autonomous work teams allocate work and determine pace, as in Sweden, and also manage maintenance, quality control, engineering, personnel and custodial services. The company tries to combine dull jobs with challenging ones, and the employee is paid according to the number of different jobs he has learned to do. Elected team leaders have replaced management supervisors; management itself does not make factory rules. The company gives the teams the economic information needed to make decisions traditionally made on higher levels.

There is little question that the Topeka system is a success. In some of its other plants General Foods had been troubled by frequent shutdowns, product waste and even sabotage, but in the Topeka factory wastage has been drastically reduced and shutdowns are rare. In fact, 40 per cent fewer workers are needed to run the plant than the engineers had estimated. Even more significant is the employees' attitude. One boiler operator explained: "Everything that goes on here, we do it.... Moving from job to job makes you more alert. I get a kind of joy out of it because it's challenging.... General Foods puts responsibility on me, and I can accept it."

Other attempts to overcome work alienation involve flexibility—both of time and of careers. In West Germany, for example, about 3,500 business organizations have adopted some form of "sliding time" to permit employees to choose their own work hours. Under this system, the firms' doors are open from 7 a.m. to 7 p.m. and workers show up whenever they want—as long as they are on the job during the "core time" from 10 a.m. to 3 p.m., and put in a 40-hour week. Polaroid Corporation in Cambridge, Massachusetts, offers its employees a more permanent choice. If they want, Polaroid workers can try out for different jobs in the company for three months; their old jobs are held open during this time and they are paid their regular salary. Most do return to their former slots, but a few end up with entirely new careers. One janitor, for example, ended up with a permanent job as a writer in the communications department.

All such experiments, of course, as well as the new organizational theories, must be evaluated with caution. After all, only 80 persons work at the General Foods plant in Topeka, a tiny fraction of the company's total 47,000-person labor force. Volvo's revolutionary factory turns out some 100 cars a day; General Motors' Lordstown plant produces 101 an hour. Some of the new strategies may work in the long run, and some may not. They may cost more—in terms of dollars and entrenched attitudes—than many organizations are willing to pay.

Perhaps the real solution to job alienation is the recognition that the importance of work itself is changing for many people today. "People look at work in different ways than they used to," says Douglas Fraser, vice president of the United Automobile Workers. Indeed, a 1974 survey by Daniel Yankelovich found that only 56 per cent of the workers under 25 believed that "hard work pays off," compared with 79 per cent four years earlier. The old 19th Century values and practices that still reign over many organizations are being cast aside by new technology, affluence—and attitudes. "Workers want control over their destiny," says R. W. Revans, an industrial consultant in Brussels and former manpower chief for the British Coal Board. "We are now part of a changing social ethic. If leaderships are going to go on existing, they must do so by persuasion, not power. This means compromise, consensus, negotiation. Instead of authority we must think in terms of negotiation." Such negotiation, of course, is bound to end with a greater emphasis on the worth of the individual, and on the demands of the human spirit. When, as and if things turn out that way, big organizations will never be the same.

Bibliography

†*Available only in paperback.*
**Also available in paperback.*

*Argyris, Chris, *Personality and Organization*. Harper & Row Publishers, Inc., 1957.

*Baltzell, E. Digby, *The Protestant Establishment: Aristocracy and Caste in America*. Random House, Inc., 1964.

*Barnard, Chester I., *The Functions of the Executive*. Harvard University Press, 1962.

†Bell, Gerald, ed., *Organizations and Human Behavior*. Prentice-Hall, Inc., 1967.

*Blau, Peter M., *The Dynamics of Bureaucracy*. University of Chicago Press, 1955.

†Burger, Chester, *Creative Firing: Why Management Firings Happen and How to Reduce Them*. Crowell Collier & Macmillan, Inc., 1973.

†*Executive Etiquette*. Crowell Collier & Macmillan, Inc., 1969.

Casson, Lionel, *Ancient Egypt*. TIME-LIFE BOOKS, 1965.

†Chinoy, Ely, *Automobile Workers and the American Dream*. Beacon Press, 1965.

†Cottrell, Leonard, *The Anvil of Civilization*. New American Library Inc., 1957.

†Dalton, Gene W., and Paul R. Lawrence, eds., *Motivation and Control in Organizations*. Richard D. Irwin, Inc., 1971.

Dalton, Melville, *Men Who Manage*. John Wiley & Sons, Inc., 1961.

Davis, Keith, *Human Behavior at Work: Human Relations and Organizational Behavior*. McGraw-Hill Book Co., 1972.

†DeCamp, L. Sprague, *The Ancient Engineers*. M.I.T. Press, 1970.

Drucker, Peter, *Men, Ideas & Politics*. Harper & Row Publishers, Inc., 1971.

Dubin, Robert, *The World of Work: Industrial Society and Human Relations*. Prentice-Hall, Inc., 1958.

*Edwards, I. E., *The Pyramids of Egypt*. Viking Press, Inc., 1972.

†Etzioni, Amitai, *A Comparative Analysis of Complex Organizations*. Free Press, 1971.

*Fairbank, John K., *The U.S. and China*. Harvard University Press, 1971.

Fakhry, Ahmed, *The Pyramids*. University of Chicago Press, 1969.

Frankel, Charles, *High on Foggy Bottom: An Outsider's Inside View of the Government*. Harper & Row Publishers, Inc., 1969.

*Gerth, Hans H., and C. Wright Mills, *From Max Weber: Essays in Sociology*. Oxford University Press, 1946.

†Goffman, Erving, *The Presentation of Self in Everyday Life*. Doubleday & Co., Inc., 1959.

*Gouldner, Alvin, *Patterns of Industrial Democracy: A Case Study of Modern Factory Administration*. Free Press, 1954.

*Harrington, Alan, *Life in the Crystal Palace*. Alfred A. Knopf, Inc., 1959.

Heller, Robert, *The Great Executive Dream*. Delacorte Press, 1972.

Heyer, Carl, *The Encyclopedia of Management*. Van Nostrand Reinhold Company, 1973.

Homans, George C., *The Human Group*. Harcourt, Brace & World, Inc., 1950.

Jay, Antony, *Corporation Man*. Random House, Inc., 1971.

Jenkins, David, *Job Power: Blue and White Collar Democracy*. Doubleday & Co., Inc., 1973.

Lewis, Naphtali, and Meyer Reinhold, eds., *The Roman Civilization*. Columbia University Press, 1955.

†Luthans, Fred, *Contemporary Readings in Organizational Behavior*. McGraw-Hill Book Co., 1972.

*Malamud, Bernard, *A New Life*. Farrar, Straus & Giroux, Inc., 1961.

Marsh, R. M., *The Mandarins*. Free Press, 1961.

Mayo, Elton, *The Human Problems of an Industrial Civilization*. The Macmillan Co., 1939.

Montross, Lynn, *War Through the Ages*. Harper & Row Publishers, Inc., 1960.

Moore, Wilbert E., *The Conduct of the Corporation*. Random House, Inc., 1962.

†Muhlen, Norbert, *The Incredible Krupps*. Universal Publishing & Distributing Corp., 1969.

†Nakane, Chie, *Human Relations in Japan*. Ministry of Foreign Affairs, 1972.

*Packard, Vance, *The Status Seekers*. David McKay Co., Inc., 1959.

Parker, Henry D., *The Roman Legions*. Barnes & Noble Books, 1971.

*Parkinson, C. Northcote, *Parkinson's Law*. Houghton Mifflin Co., 1957.

Peter, Laurence F., and Raymond Hull, *The Peter Principle*. William Morrow & Co., Inc., 1969.

†Presthus, Robert, *The Organizational Society*. Alfred A. Knopf, Inc., 1962.

Reischauer, Edwin, and John K. Fairbank, *East Asia: The Great Tradition*. Houghton Mifflin Co., 1960.

Roethlisberger, F. L., and William J.

Dickson, *Management and the Worker.* Harvard University Press, 1939.
†Rose, Peter, ed., *The Study of Society, An Integrated Anthology.* Random House, Inc., 1973.
Rothschild, Emma, *Paradise Lost: The Decline of the Auto-Industrial Age.* Random House, Inc., 1973.
†Ruitenbeck, Hendrik, ed., *The Dilemma of Organizational Society.* E. P. Dutton & Co., Inc., 1963.
Seidenberg, Robert, *Corporate Wives—Corporate Casualties?* American Management Associations, Inc., 1973.
†Service, Elman, *The Hunters.* Prentice-Hall, Inc., 1966.

Shostak, Arthur B., and William Gomberg, *Blue Collar World.* Prentice-Hall, Inc., 1965.
Sloan, Alfred P., Jr., *My Years With General Motors.* Doubleday & Co., Inc., 1964.
Stewart, Desmond, *The Pyramids and Sphinx.* Newsweek, 1971.
Strauss, George, and Leonard R. Sayles, *Personnel: The Human Problems of Management.* Prentice-Hall, Inc., 1967.
†Tarnowieski, Dale, *The Changing Success Ethic.* American Management Associations, Inc., 1973.
Taylor, Frederick W., *Scientific Management.* Greenwood Press, Inc., 1947.

Terkel, Studs, *Working: People Talk About What They Do All Day and How They Feel About What They Do.* Pantheon Books, Inc., 1974.
*Tiger, Lionel, *Men in Groups.* Random House, Inc., 1969.
*Toffler, Alvin, *Future Shock.* Random House, Inc., 1972.
*Whyte, William H., Jr., *The Organization Man.* Simon and Schuster, Inc., 1956.
†*Work in America.* Report of a Special Task Force to the Secretary of Health, Education and Welfare. M.I.T. Press, 1972.
Zweig, Ferdynand, *The Worker in an Affluent Society.* Free Press, 1961.

Picture Credits

The sources for the illustrations in this book are shown below. Credits from left to right are separated by semicolons, from top to bottom by dashes.

Cover—Jay Maisel. 6—Robert Walch. 10—Dmitri Kessel from TIME-LIFE Picture Agency. 11—Francisco Erize from Bruce Coleman—Douglas Faulkner; Alfred Eisenstaedt from TIME-LIFE Picture Agency. 14—Tony Howarth from Woodfin Camp and Associates. 17—Derek Bayes, courtesy British Museum. 18—Brian Brake from Rapho Guillumette. 20—The Bettmann Archive. 21—Lewis W. Hine, courtesy International Museum of Photography at George Eastman House. 24, 25—Robert Brigham from TIME-LIFE Picture Agency. 26, 27—Co Rentmeester from TIME-LIFE Picture Agency. 28, 29—Nick Wheeler from Black Star. 30, 31—Neal Slavin. 32, 33—Carlo Bavagnoli from TIME-LIFE Picture Agency. 34—Lewis W. Hine, courtesy International Museum of Photography at George Eastman House. 38—George Krause. 40—Henri Dauman. 43 through 46—Thomas Höpker from Woodfin Camp and Associates. 50—Claude Perez, Paris. 54 through 63—Osamu Murai. 64—Wolf von dem Bussche. 68—*Seattle Times.* 71 through 74—David Lees. 76—Juan Guzman. 78 through 83—Aldo Durazzi. 84—Copyright Vojta Dukat. 88, 89—Henry Grossman for FORTUNE, © 1967 Time Inc. 90, 91, 92—Howard Sochurek. 93—NASA. 94, 95—Ralph Morse from TIME-LIFE Picture Agency. 96, 97—Ralph Morse from TIME-LIFE Picture Agency; NASA. 98, 99—Edwin Aldrin, NASA. 100—Gene Laurents. 104—Western Electric. 105—Wide World. 109—Edward Hausner, *The New York Times.* 112—Friedman-Abeles. 114, 115—© 1974, *The Washington Monthly.* 118—Wide World. 120 through 127—Drawings by Robert Osborn. 128—No credit. 132—Dick Frank. 134, 135—Courtesy Richard C. Brinckerhoff family. 139, 140, 141—Marvin Lichtner. 142—Terence Spencer. 145—Tony Howarth from Woodfin Camp and Associates. 148—Margaret Bourke-White, courtesy Margaret Bourke-White Estate. 153—United Press International. 156—Leonard Freed. 158, 159—Brown Brothers. 161—United Artists. 162—United Press International. 165—Courtesy Volvo. 166, 167, 168—Jean Hermansson.

Index

Numerals in italics indicate a photograph or drawing of the subject mentioned.

A

Absenteeism, 150, 164, 169, 170
Academic organization(s): influence of over private lives, 130; titles in, 41
Advancement, *126*; assessment games for, 49; key to, 79-80; in military organizations, 75; opportunity of production workers for, 157-160; personality evaluations for, 48-49; tests for, 48
Agriculture, and ancient organizations, 9
Alcohol, 161
Aldrin, Edwin, *95*
Alienation, 8, 149-171; advancement opportunities and, 157-160; of assembly-line workers, 150, 157; attempted solutions to, 150, 163-171; and automation, 157; of blue-collar workers, 152; costs of, 160-163; education and, 152; effect of television on, 155; of executives, 154; flexibility and, 171; and health, 161; and hierarchy of needs, 154-155; job enrichment and, 164-171; lack of, in Japan, 163; of manual workers, 150; in underdeveloped countries, 155, 163; of white-collar workers, 152-154
Alston, G. Cyprian, 20
Amory, Cleveland, 36
Animal organization(s), 8, *10-11*
Ant(s), 10
Apartment(s), company-provided: in Japan, 60, *61*; as perquisite, in Europe, 130, 136
Apollo, Project. *See* Moon landing
Arkwright, Richard, 20; spinner invented by, *20*
Armstrong, Neil, *95*, *98-99*
Assembly line(s): alienation on, 157; in Charlie Chaplin film, *161*; at General Motors' Lordstown plant, 160; humanizing, 150, 164, *165-168*, 169-171; in Japanese company, 57; of Model T Fords, *158-159*; in underdeveloped countries, 152, 155
Astronaut(s), training of, *94*, *95*
Authority, depersonalization of, 38-39, 65-67; division of, 75-76; of early river kings, 9-10
Automation, 55, 87, 157

B

Backalenick, Irene, 136
Bakhtiaris, *14*, 15
Bay of Pigs, as groupthink, 81, 82
Beating the system: forms of, 111-113; risks in, 113-116
Black Palace, *76*, 77
Blake, William, 151
Blanchard, Francis, 150
Blau, Peter, 108, 113
Boredom, 150, 154, *156*, 157
Bottleneck(s), 111-113
Bourguiba, Habib, *50*, 51
Boyd, Alan, 85
Brennan, Peter, 163
Brinckerhoff, Barbara and Richard, *134-135*
Brownson, Orestes, 129
Bureaucracy(ies): agricultural, 9-12; ancient, 9-17; of ancient China, 16-17, 18; of ancient Egypt, 12, 13-15; of British Admiralty, 77; definition of, 23; in France, 77; functions of, 9-12, 22; history of, 9-17; importance of writing in, 12-13, 15-16; in Italy, 77; need for, 9-12; of New York City Police Department, 77; resistance of Inner Face in, 111; of river societies, 9-16; Roman Catholic Church as, 19-20; in Roman Empire, 19; in Soviet Union, 77; top-heaviness of, 77-78; written records in, 12-13
Burger, Chester, 37, 49, 51

C

Caesar, Augustus, 17
Carnegie, Andrew, 145
Cartwright, Ian, *139*
Cartwright, Patricia, *139-142*
Chain of command, 65, 67
Chaplin, Charlie, *161*
Chase Manhattan Bank, 42
Chevalier, Michael, 129
China, ancient: administrative hierarchy of, 16; examination halls of, *18*; examination system of, 16-17
Chrysler, Walter P., 65
Chrysler Corporation, 65, 90
Church, Roman Catholic: badges of rank in, 41; Benedictine Order of, 19-20; ceremonial displays of, *32-33*; Cistercian monks of, *71-74*; division in pyramidal structure of, 67; functions of, 19; hierarchy of, 19; as oldest living complex organization, 19; rules of, 19-20; titles in, 41
Cistercian monks, *71-74*; routine of, 72; rules of, 71
Classification of organization(s): coercive, 67-68; normative, 67, 68; utilitarian, 67, 68-69
Coercive organization(s), 67-68, 70, 76, 77
Communication(s): as aid to adaptability of organization, 87; with boss, 85-86; channels of, 75, 83, 87; to combat alienation, 164; downward, 83; extensive, 84-85; feedback of, 83-84; through gatekeeper, 86-87; by grapevine, 116-118, *124*; of Inner Face, 116-118; interoffice memoranda, *114-115*; methods of, 83; open-door policy as, 85-86; purposes of, 83, 164; by two-way funnel, 117, *124-125*; upward, 83-84; written, need for, 7

Company town(s), 129
Compatibility, social, 108-110
Compliance, nature of, 66, 67-69
Concentration camp(s), 67-68
Confidence, as key to advancement, 79-80
Control, coordinated central, 66
Corning Glass Company, 164
Corporation(s), business: division of authority in, 75-76; function of, 7; highly diversified, 87; line personnel in, 75; multinational, 87, 147; span of control in, 76-77; staff personnel in, 75
Correctional institutions, 68
Cottrell, Leonard, 12
Cunningham, Walter, *94*
Curtice, Harlow, 144

D

Davis, Keith, 103, 116, 117, 119
Decision(s): communication of, 66, 83; by consensus, 82-83; by groupthink, 80-82; importance of, 65-66, 79-83
DeLorean, John, 144
Display(s): as celebration(s) of organization(s), *24-33*; Electrolux convention as, *30-31*; International Olympics as, *26-27*; Iranian anniversary celebration as, *28-29*; of medieval guilds, 24; of Roman Catholic Church, *32-33*; of Roman legions, 19, 24; of Soviet government, *24-25*
Donations, *125*
Douglas Aircraft, 92
Drugs, 161
Dubin, Robert, 103-104
Durant, William C., 65, 66
Dutch Army, *162*, 163
Dyer, William G., 130

E

Eaton Corporation, 170
Education: and compatibility, 108; increase in, and discontent, 152; for white-collar workers, 153-154
Efficiency, studies of: in automated plants, 69, 70; and Inner Face, 105-107; and lighting, 104-105; in research laboratories, 69-70
Efficiency, Frederick W. Taylor's doctrine of, 22, 152
Ego needs, 155
Egypt, ancient: as agricultural organization, 9-12; building of pyramids in, 13-14, 87; civilization in, 12; organization of, 12, 13; written records in, 12-13, 17
Electrolux Company, convention of, *30-31*
Entertaining, 146, 147
Escapism, 161
Etzioni, Amitai, 67
Experience, shared, 108, 110
Extracurricular activity(ies): civic work as,

146; educational courses as, 144; golf as, 130, *145*; helpful to advancement, 145; of Matsushita Company of Japan, *58-59*; philanthropy as, 130, 146

F

Factory organization(s): garment factory, *21*; and Industrial Revolution, 20-21; job satisfaction in, 130, 155; management of, 22; Ruskin's description of workers in, 151; Adam Smith's views of, 21, 151; Taylor's doctrine of efficiency for, 22, 152
Fairbank, John King, 12
Fan Chung-yen, 16
Federal decentralization, 65-66, 87
Feedback, of communications, 83-84
Firestone Tire and Rubber, 47
Firing techniques, 51-52
Flexibility, of working hours, 171
Frankel, Charles, 110
Fraser, Douglas, 171
Fusilier fish, 10, *11*

G

Gaius, Marius, 17
Gallup Poll, 161
Gay, Hobart R., 116
General Foods Corporation, 170-171
General Motors Corporation: corporate friendships in, 144; early history of, 65; groupthink in, 81; Lordstown factory of, 160, 171; organization study of, by Sloan, 65-66; Sloan addressing workmen of, *68*, *69*
Gilbreth, Frank and Lillian, 152, *153*
Golf, 130, *145*
Government organization(s): British, 8; functions of, 7, 22; Inner Face in, 101, 108, 110-111; interoffice memoranda of, *114-115*; red tape of, *78-83*; salaries in, 47; study of, by Blau, 108; Weber's analysis of, 23
Grace, W. R., Corporation, 84-85
Gränges AE, 170
Great Wall of China, 87
Group(s), informal, 101, 106
Groupthink: dangers of, 80-81; as decision-making process, 80; examples of, in America, 81-82
Grumman Corporation, 92

H

Haldeman, H. R., 86
Harrington, Alan, 52, 53
Harvard Business Review, 78
Hawthorne investigation(s), *104*-107
Health, Education and Welfare, U.S. Department of, 149, 152, 155
Health, effect of alienation on, 161
Herodotus, 12
Herzberg, Frederick, 164
Honeywell, 91

Hospital(s): feedback in, 84; operation in, *38*, *39*; types of authority in, 70
Housing, company-provided: in Japan, 60, *61*; as perquisite, in Europe, 130, 136
How to Succeed in Business without Really Trying, *112*, 113
Human relations movement, 163-164
Human societies, early, 8-9, 15

I

IBM, 47, 53, 137; assembly line at typewriter plant of, 170; open-door policy of, 85
Illinois Central Railroad, 85
Imperial Chemical Industries Limited, 169
Incompetence, level of, 78-79
Individual(s): in early societies, 8-9; in factory organizations, 22; in modern organizational society, 9, 23, 48
Industrial Revolution, 20-21, 87, 151; factory evolved from, *21*
Inner Face, 101-119; authority of, 101, 102; beating the system by, 111-113; as conservative force, 118-119; control of production by, 106-107; definition of, 101-102; discipline of, 106-107; efficiency of, 111-113; at high levels, 102-103, 110; human need for, 103; humanizing effect of, 113; informal work group as part of, 101-102; at lower levels, 103; loyalty to, 108, 110; Mitsubishi Group of Japan as, 102-103; ostracism by, 107, 109; power of, 102, 107, 116; punishment by, 107-108; resistance of, 111; risks of, 113-116; rituals of, 118-119; social compatibility in, 108-110; studies of, 104-107; systems of procedure as part of, 102; tension between formal structure and, 103, 110; unofficial rules as part of, 102
Insects, organized, 10
Institute for Social Research, University of Michigan, 161
Iranian soldiers, *28-29*

J

Japanese corporation(s): benefits given by, 53; business entertaining in, 146-147; decision by consensus in, 82-83; dependence of members on, 53; influence of, over members' lives, 129; lack of alienation in, 163; loyalty of employees to, 53, 150, 163; similarity of, to family, 163
Jay, Antony, 117
Jenkins, David, 152
Job enrichment, 164-171; on assembly lines, 164, 170; flexibility as, 171; teamwork production method as, 169-170; in white-collar work, 164-169; worker management as, 170
Joseph, 15
Josephus, 19

K

Kafka, Franz, 152
Kaiser Industries, 144
Kennedy, John F., 78, 82, 88, 101
Kennedy, Robert, 82
Kiev, Ari, 85-86, 136, 138
Knudsen, Semon, 144
Krupp, Alfred, 35

L

Labovitz, George, 131
Langur(s), *11*
Lecumberri Prison, *76*, *77*
Lefevre, Mike, 149
Line personnel: authority of, 75-76; conflict of, with staff personnel, 70, 75; in U.S. Army, 70-75
Lockwood, David, 48
Lowell factory system, 129
Loyalty(ies): in ancient river organizations, 12, 15; of combat soldier, 108; loss of, through alienation, 161; sources of, 108; of staff men, 75

M

Malamud, Bernard, 119
Management-improvement sessions, 164
Marine Corps, U.S., training for, *43-46*
Maslow, Abraham, 155
Mass production factory, *21*
Matsushita Electric Industrial Company: automation in, 55; company life in, *54-63*; company stores of, *61*; company-owned housing of, 60, *61*; corporate rituals in, 54-55; employee benefits in, 55; employee loyalty in, 55; factory(ies) in, *54-55*, *56*, *57*; family plan of, 61; job security in, 55; marriage arrangements by, 60, *61*; recreation facilities of, *58-59*, *62-63*
Mayo, Elton, 104, *105*, 163
Medical staff(s), hospital, 68, 70
Medical team, *38*, *39*
Memoranda, interoffice, *114-115*
Menes, 12
Mental hospitals, 67
Merton, Robert, 47
Military Academy, U.S., 107, 109
Military organization(s): of ancient Egypt, 13; badges on clothing in, 41; British Admiralty, 77; British Army, 119, 139-142; distinction between line and staff in, 70-75; division, horizontal, in structure of, 67; Dutch Army, *162*, 163; fullness in, 67; influence of, over private life styles, 130; Iranian Army, *28-29*; perquisites of rank in, 41; regulations of, 163; role of British officer's wife in, *139-142*; Roman army, 17-19, 24; salaries in, 47; systems of compliance used by, 69; titles in, 41; U.S. Marine Corps, training for, *43-46*

175

Mission Control, 97. *See also* Moon landing
Mitsubishi Group, 77, 102-103
Mobile(s), secure, 51
Montgomery Ward, 136
Moon landing: accomplishment of, 97, *98-99*
Moore, Wilbert, 37, 47, 49, 51, 117, 131
Morgan, J. P., 145
Motorola Corporation, 164

N
Nakane, Chie, 62, 163
NASA (National Aeronautics and Space Administration), 88, 91, 92, 94, 97. *See also* Moon landing
National Industrial Recreation Association, 144
Nixon, Richard M., 86, 119
Nord, Walter R., 164
Normative organization(s), 67, 68, 69-70, 71

O
Olympics, International, *26-27*
Open-door policy, 85-86
Organizational structure(s): absence of, 87; of ancient civilizations, 9-13, 15, 16-17; federal decentralization as, 65-66, 87; feudalism in, 131; generations of, 87; horizontal, 87; multinational diversified corporations as, 87; need for, 7; personal management by entrepreneur as, 21-22, 87; pyramidal, 65-66, 67, 87; of Roman army, 17-19
Osborn, Robert, drawings by, *120-127*
Ostracism, 68, 106-107, 109

P
Page, Charles, 101
Parkinson, C. Northcote, 77
Parkinson's Law, 77, 79; definition of, 77
Participatory management, 163-164
Patton, George S., 116
Pearl Harbor, as groupthink, 81-82
Pelosi, James J., *109*
Penguin(s), *11*
Perquisite(s) (perks): in Europe, 130, 133-136; in military organizations, 41; tax-free, 133-136
Peter, Laurence J., 78
Peter Principle, 78-79; definition of, 78
Philanthropy, 146
Polaroid Corporation, 171
Pompidou, Georges, 150
Pope Paul VI, *32-33*
Pravda, 150
Prison(s), 67, 76, 77
Private life(ves), effect of organization(s) on, 129-147; of blue-collar families, 138-143; in choice of friends, 130, 143-144; in Japan, 53, 54, *58-63*, 129, 130; in transfers, 130, *134-135*, 136-138

Productivity: determination of, by Inner Face, 106-107; of General Motors Lordstown plant, 160, 171; investigations of, 104-107; of Model T assembly line, 165; of Volvo plant, 165, 171
Pyramid(s), of Egypt, 13-15, 87
Pyramidal structure: division of authority within, 75-76; Inner Face within, 101; Sloan's plan for, 65-67; spans of control in, 76-77

R
Raikin, Arkady, 77
Rank, 12, 39-41, 42, *50*, 51
Raytheon Company, 144
Record(s), written, 12-13
Red tape, for marriage, *78-83*
Religious organization(s): in ancient Egypt, 13, 17; badges on clothing in, 41; influence of, over private life styles, 130; titles in, 41. *See also* Church, Roman Catholic
Renault automobile factory, 150
Resort(s), *62-63*
Revans, R. W., 171
Reynolds, Russell, 131
Robots, 160
Rousseau, 68
Ruskin, John, 151

S
Saab, 169
St. Benedict, 19-20, 71
Sargent, William Clay, 154
Sartre, Jean-Paul, 36-37
Saturn rocket, *90*
Schwab, Charles M., 145
Scientific management, 152
Scribe(s), 12, 13, 15-16
Secure mobile(s), 51
Security, as need, 155
Seidenberg, Robert, 133, 137, 138, 147
Self-fulfillment, as need, 155
Sensitivity-training movement, 164
Silence, The, 109
Sliding time, 171
Sloan, Alfred P., 68, 69, 76
Smith, Adam, 21, 151
Smith, Harvey L., 70
Social Security headquarters, U.S., *40*, 41
Soviet Union: anniversary celebration of, *24-25*; top-heavy bureaucracy of, 77-78
Staff personnel, 70-75; authority of, 75-76; loyalties of, 75; professional expertise of, 75
Standard Operating Procedure (SOP), 37
State Department, U.S., 42, 110, 113
Status symbol(s), 42-47, 68, 69
Stewart, Desmond, 15
Strainer(s), 51
System, the, 7-8

T
"T" group(s), 164
Task force(s), 87, *104*, 105. *See also* Moon landing
Tea Tasters, U.S. Board of Federal, *118*, 119
Television, 155
Terkel, Studs, 113, 149, 161
Texas Instruments Corporation, 170
Time-and-motion study, 152
Toffler, Alvin, 87, 136
Towne, Henry, 22
Transfer(s), 130, *134-135*, 136-138; adaptations to, *134-135*, 137-138; of blue-collar families, 138; effect of, on family, *134-135*, 136; in Europe, 136; stress of, for wife, 137
Tribal council(s), as organization, *14*, 15

U
Uni, 15
Unimates, 160
United Automobile Workers, 161
U.S. Steel Corporation, 145
Utilitarian organization(s), 67, 68-69, 70

V
Vacation(s), company-provided, *62-63*, 130
Vespasian, 19
Volvo, 169-170, 171; assembly teams of, *165-168*
Volvox, 10

W
Wall Street Journal, 154
Washington Monthly, The, 115
Watson, Thomas J., Sr., 85
Weber, Max, 23
Western Electric Company Hawthorne plant: relay assembly room of, *104*, 105; study of, 104-107
Whitman, Walt, 149
Whyte, William H., Jr., 38, 131, 132, 133, 143
Wife(ves): of British Army officer, *139-142*; and choice of friends, 143; economic competition with, 133; in Europe, 133; influence of corporate life on, 131; in Japan, 147; loneliness of, 132; qualities of, 131; role of, 131, 146; screening of, 131; sexual competition for, 133; in transfers, *134-135*, 136, 137-138
Wildebeest(s), *10*
Williamson, D. T. N., 157
Writing, 13
Written record(s), ancient Egyptian, 17

Y
Yankelovich, Daniel, 171

Z
Zaibatsu, 102-103

Printed in U.S.A.